Duane Shinn's

Secrets of Piano Chords & P

The Secret Backdoor to Exciting Piano Playing

Shinn Trading Inc.

edicated to my buddy and pal Bev, who is also the love of my life.

Table of Contents

. . . .Chords

I wish you could have seen me play the piano when I was just learning. I was the nearest thing to "hopeless" that you could imagine. I was into baseball, not music – and my heroes were Joe DiMaggio, Mickey Mantle, and Ted Williams. (And by the way, I *still* have a picture of those 3 guys on my wall.) My dream was to hit baseballs like them, not to play the piano.

Formal training is fine *if* you have the time and money. But most adults don't want to wait forever before they can play something enjoyable on the piano. I took lessons when I was a kid, but found it boring. Not only that, but all I could do was play the written music exactly as it was written. **Without the sheet music in front of me, I didn't have a clue what to do.** So I lost interest in piano playing.

But shortly after that, I had the opportunity to play in a school combo -- but to do that, I had to learn chords, and learn them fast. Seems the piano player of the group had graduated the previous year, and nobody else played piano well enough to play in the school jazz combo. I didn't know zilch about playing in a group, and I didn't know chords. But I was excited to have the opportunity to play with older guys, and so I took the job.

The lead sax player told me I really should know chords in order to play in the group, so I searched through a music magazine until I found an ad for a chord chart. It cost two bucks, as I recall, so I sent off for it. When I received it in the mail I slipped it behind the keys on my parents old upright piano, and promptly learned to play my first chord – **Dm7**. I *LOVED* the sound of it, and was hooked for life on chords. The 2nd chord I learned was **Cmaj7**, then **Em7**, then **Ebm7** – and before that first night was over I had learned to play "*Frankie & Johnnie*" – the tune in my right hand, and those fabulous 7th chords in my left hand!

Talk about excited! Within a few weeks I could play dozens of songs using chords. And I discovered that my sight-reading speed greatly improved at the same time, because **now I understood what I was seeing** on the printed page.

I loved it – **LOVED IT** – ***LOVED IT!*** And it even sounded good enough to impress some of my friends the next day. I suppose that simple chord chart that cost me two bucks has been worth several million over the course of my lifetime. And much more than that, has been worth quadrillions in pleasure and satisfaction and relaxation and……

Chords are a way in to the world of piano playing ***without*** *having to go through the front door: years and years of scales, drills, rote practicing, etc. Chords are really a* ***shortcut to understanding*** *and playing music without all the formal training. So I came in through the* ***back door*** *instead, and now I enjoy what I used to hate!*

Why?

Because I understand what I'm doing because now I understand chords and chord progressions. I eventually went on to get my Masters Degree -- and it was easy because of all I had learned about music theory and harmony due to playing and understanding chords.

Even though I came in the back door as far as piano playing was concerned, I learned fast because of what I knew about chords, so college was a snap, and so was my post-graduate Masters Degree at Southern Oregon University. After high school I studied with several of the finest private teachers on the West Coast, including a year with THE finest teacher – his name was Dave – and his studio was on Cauhenga Blvd. in Hollywood. As I would come for my piano lesson, I would often pass a big name recording artist coming to their lesson – and anyone who was anyone in Hollywood in those days took lessons from Dave.

Dave taught me 2 fundamental principles about piano playing:

1. The piano *is NOT* played with the hands – it is played with the **brain**. The hands are just *tools*.

2. If you master **chord relationships**, you can master music.

I've got **little fat hands** with **short fingers**. Hardly the ideal hands for piano playing. I've also got a **lousy sense of rhythm** for a professional musician.

But you know what? Because of those two principles Dave taught me, I can play "above" my fat hands and my weak rhythm.

Above?

Yes.

Above.

Once a person "gets into the flow" of understanding chord relationships and then letting the brain knowledge flow into the hands, that person plays "above" his ability.

Can you do the same? That depends entirely on how bad you want it and how much time and effort you are prepared to put into it. But since I (and countless others) have done it, I don't see why you can't also.

So ***go to it***. Master each lesson as it comes, and don't skip around.

Before you realize it, you'll be playing chords with the best of 'em! And most of all, you'll be enjoying what you're doing and understanding what you're playing.

Now that's what I call fun!

What Piano Chords Do I Absolutely, Positively Have To Know?

As you probably know, there are thousands and thousands of different chords - everything from basic major chords to minor 7ths to 13ths to suspensions to poly-chords. Someday, you might want to learn all those chords if you don't already know them.

But meanwhile, there are 3 chords -- *just 3* -- that you absolutely, positively have to know. If you don't know these three, there's hardly a song in the whole world that you could play. But by knowing just 3 chords, you can play hundreds, if not thousands of songs!

Really?

Really!

Are you ready? Here they are:

I IV V

Huh? What's all that about?

Here's what:

In every key there are 3 chords -- *just 3 chords* -- which are known as "*primary chords*" -- chords that occur way more than other chords. They are like family members of that particular key. They are groups of notes built on the *1st note* of the scale, the *4th note* of that scale, and the *5th note* of that scale. (Those are 3-note chords called "*triads*" -- later we will get into 4 and 5 note chords.)

For example, here is the **C** scale on the keyboard. It runs from **C** up to **C** an octave higher. The "**I**" chord is built on the first note of the **C** scale, and so on.

So if I build a chord on the "**I**" -- every other scale note up from **C**, the chord is **C**, **E**, and **G** -- known as the "**C major chord**."

If I build a chord on the "**IV**" -- every other scale note up from **F**, the chord is **F**, **A**, and **C** -- known as the "**F major chord**."

If I build a chord on the "**V**" -- every other scale note up from **G**, the chord is **G**, **B**, and **D** -- known as the "**G major chord**."

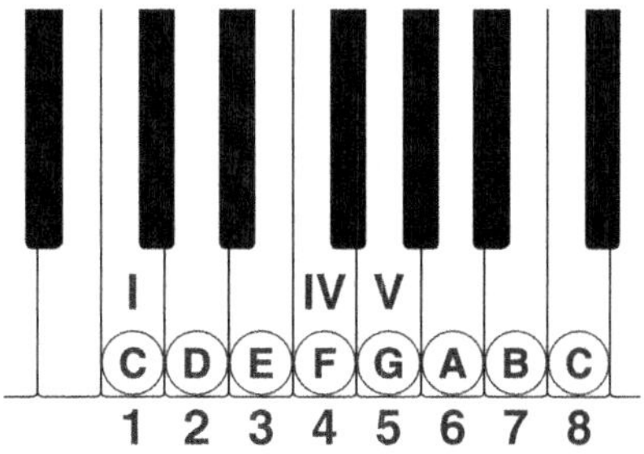

Here is what it looks like in music notation:

3 Chords You Just Gotta Know!

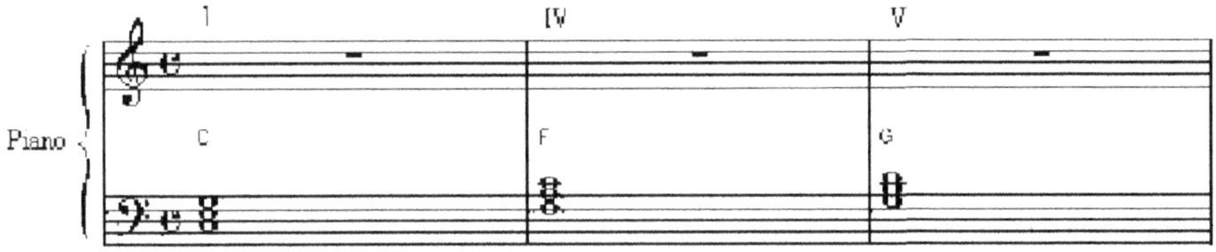

Please notice, if you haven't already, that those 3 chords contain *ALL the notes* in the **C** scale!

So what?

So any melody - tune - in the key of **C** (as long as it just uses the 8 notes of the scale) can be harmonized just by playing one of those 3 chords! Think about that -- that's a HUGE insight that most people never get.

So, in any given key you can play in, there are PRIMARY CHORDS -- chords that occur way more than other chords. They are like family members of that particular key.

At your house, let's say you have 3 people in your family -- your spouse, your child, and you. On the same block, but down the street a few houses, lives your cousin and her family. At any given moment, who are the most likely people to be in your house?

The Terminator?

Barry Bonds?

Yasser?

No sir!

I don't think so. It's possible, of course, but not too likely. If I had to guess, I would say it would be either you, your spouse, or your child. It might be your cousin down the street -- there's a much better chance of that than, say, David Letterman or Prince Charles -- but my best odds would be to guess that the family members would be there.

It's the same way with chords. In any given key, there are 3 "family members" that are residents of that key -- the **I** chord, the **IV** chord, and the **V** chord. They are far and away the most likely chords to occur in any given key.

Does that mean that there are always just 3 chords in a song? No, but there are literally hundreds of songs that are made of just 3 chords.

For example, if I am playing in the Key of C, and the first chord is the C chord and I have to guess what the next chord is, I would guess that it would be either the F chord or the G chord. Why? Because those are the other "family members." So we have narrowed the odds a great deal just by knowing who the members of the family are.

The Primary Piano Chords ("the Family") Of All the Major Keys

Here are the primary chords (the family chords) of all the major keys (remember that the primary chords are the **I** chord, the **IV** chord, and the **V** chord based on the scale of that particular key):

Key of **C**: **C, F, G**	Key of **F**: **F, Bb, C**
Key of **G**: **G, C, D**	Key of **Bb**: **Bb, Eb, F**
Key of **D**: **D, G, A**	Key of **Eb**: **Eb, Ab, Bb**
Key of **A**: **A, D, E**	Key of **Ab**: **Ab, Db, Eb**
Key of **E**: **E, A, B**	Key of **Db**: **Db, Gb, Ab**
Key of **B**: **B, E, F#**	Key of **Gb**: **Gb, Cb, Db**

Do you have to know all these chords in all these keys?

No.

You can choose to play in just one key, or just a few keys.

But what you MUST know is the 3 chords in whatever key you want to play in! That means that the stark beginner can learn 3 chords in just a few minutes, and be able to play along with thousands of tunes, because most folk songs, hymns, country songs, and many rock songs just use the 3 basic chords. That's why people who know zilch about music can pick up a guitar, learn 3 chords, and strum along while singing everything from "*On Top Of Old Smoky*" to "*Amazing Grace*" to "*My Country 'Tis Of Thee*" to "*Auld Lang Syne*" to "*Silent Night*" to..........................well, you get the idea. And not only a guitar, but a piano, keyboard, or whatever.

That's it for now.

In the next lesson we'll expand our horizons a bit, and take an overview of the types of chords available to us in addition to these 3 absolutely essential chords.

Flying Over "Chordland" Before We Land

The 48 basic piano chords times 3

Before we get down to the actual details of building chords, I would like to take you on an airplane ride over "Chordland" so you can look down and get the lay of the land -- get a good overview of how Chordland is laid out -- where the rivers and freeways and lakes and towns are, and how it all works together.

Lots of people know a few chords, but aren't sure just how many chords they need to know to cover the basics in an average song -- in other words, enough to "get along."

Sure, they would like to know how to play 9th chords and suspended 7th chords and chords built on the church modes, such as *Dorian, Lydian, Mixolydian, Aeolian, Locrian*, and so forth, but they could live without ever knowing those -- they just want to know enough chords to get by in a playing situation, from accompanying a singer at a musical to playing with a worship group at church to playing for Girl Scouts.

Well, I have *good news* for them. There are only *12 major chords*, *12 minor chords*, *12 augmented chords*, and *12 diminished chords*. That makes **48**. Then each one can be turned upside down (inverted) 3 times. Three times **48** is **144**. These are the basic 12 dozen chords a person needs to know to get along. It would sure be helpful to know how to add a 7th to a chord, but not absolutely necessary (even though it's as simple as pie!).

12 Major Piano Chords

12 Minor Piano Chords

12 Augmented Piano Chords

12 Diminished Piano Chords

48 Basic Piano Chords!

Every 3-note chord (called a triad) can be turned upside down 3 times:

Root position (name of the chord on the bottom)

1st inversion (name of the chord on top)

2nd inversion (name of the chord in the middle)

So.....

3 Inversions of Each Chord

Total = 144 Piano Chords

The second part of the good news is that **these 12 dozen chords can be learned much more quickly than most people suppose** -- it shouldn't take over an hour of concentrated practice to get somewhat of a handle on these 144 chords. Here's why:

Once a person learns the 12 major chords, all there is to finding minor and augmented chords is to move just one note from the major chord! And all there is to finding diminished chords is to move 2 notes from the major chord.

In the next lesson we'll cover all of the 12 major chords.

All The Major Piano Chords

In the last lesson, we took an "airplane ride" over Chordland just to get the lay of the land -- an overview of the world of chords.

In this lesson you will see how easy it is to learn *ALL the major chords* (there are 12 of them), and be able to play them in *seconds* -- not hours or days or weeks or months or years.

Some people go through their entire lives not being sure about what such and such a *major chord* is -- and it's all so unnecessary. You can memorize them in just a few minutes, and learn to play them in 12 seconds or less - one second per major chord. I have had *many* private students over the years who could play them all in as little as 5 seconds.

One young girl (she was about 12 at the time) had particularly fast hands, and could play them in - believe it or not - 3 seconds! I have slow hands with fat fingers, and yet I can play them in something like 5 or 6 seconds. So if I can do it with little fat hands and chubby short fingers, you can too!

First, here's what the major chords look like on the staff:

All 12 of the Major Chords!

And here's what major chords look like when played on the piano with your left hand:

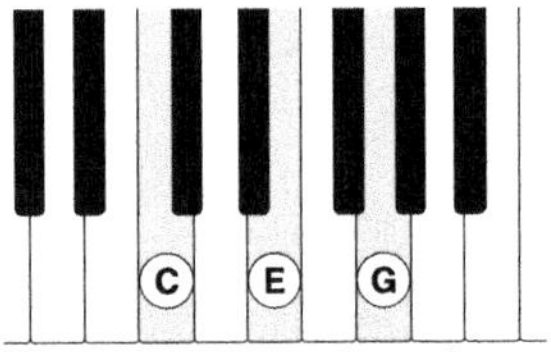

C Major Chord

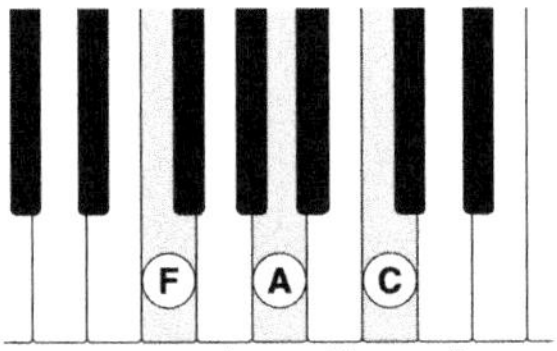

F Major Chord

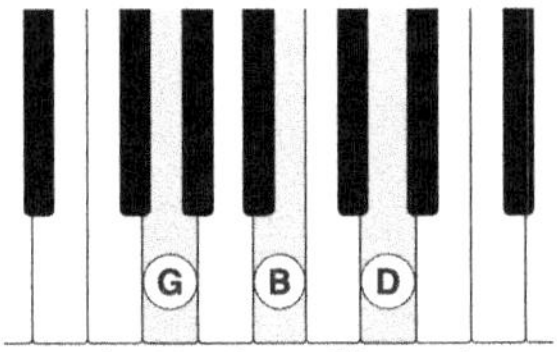

G Major Chord

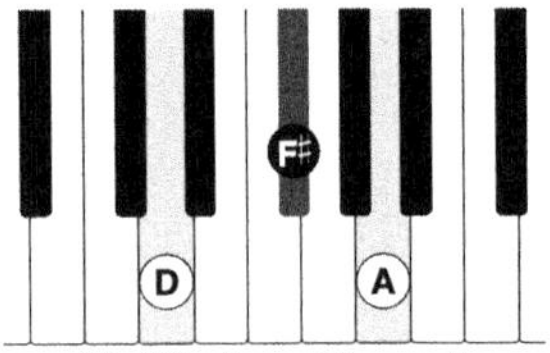

D Major Chord

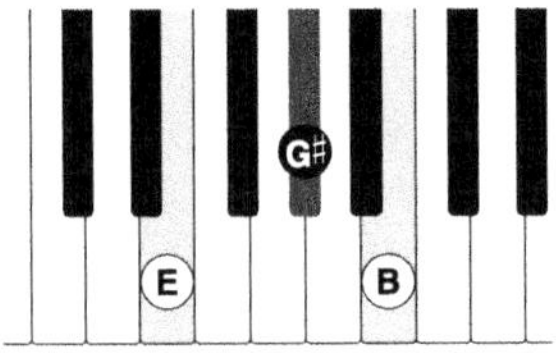

E Major Chord

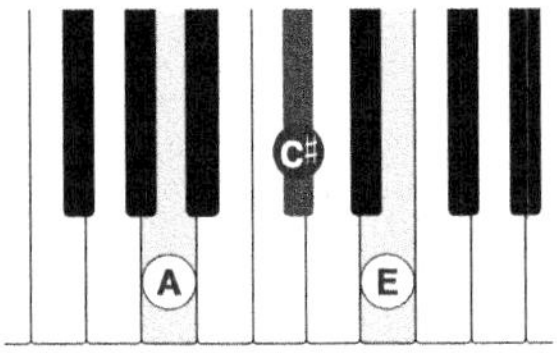

A Major Chord

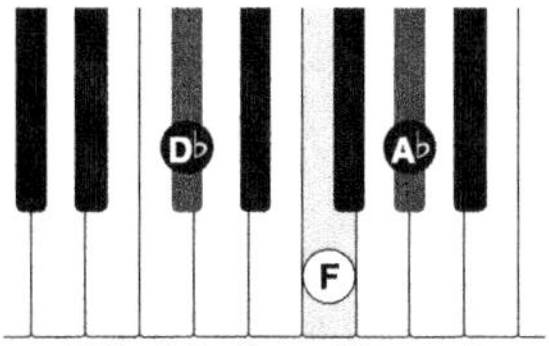

Db Major Chord

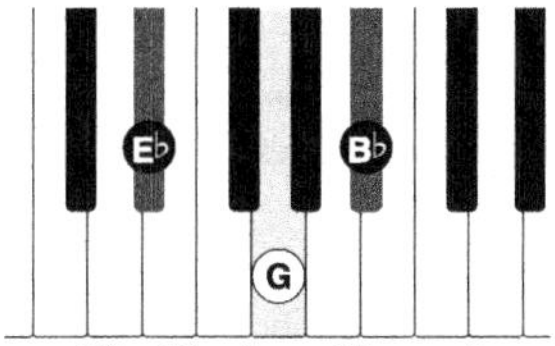

Eb Major Chord

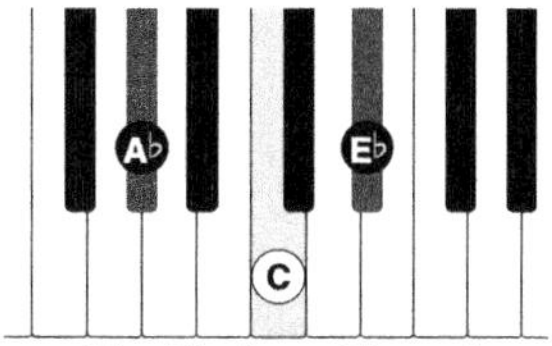

Ab Major Chord

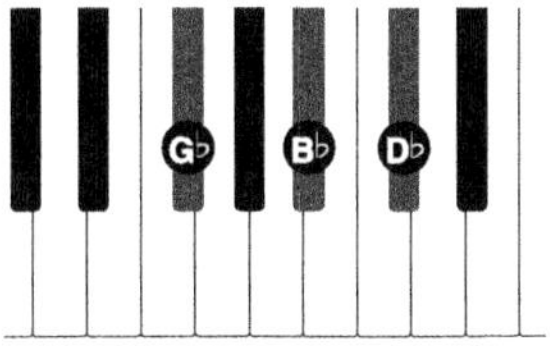

Gb Major Chord

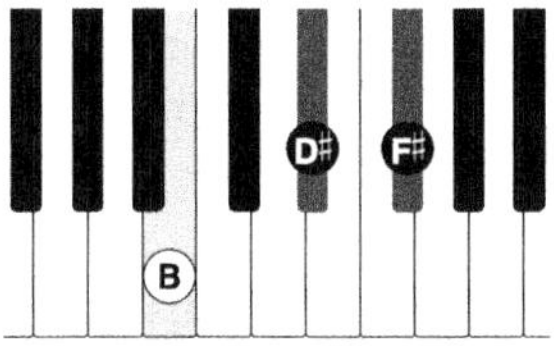

B Major Chord

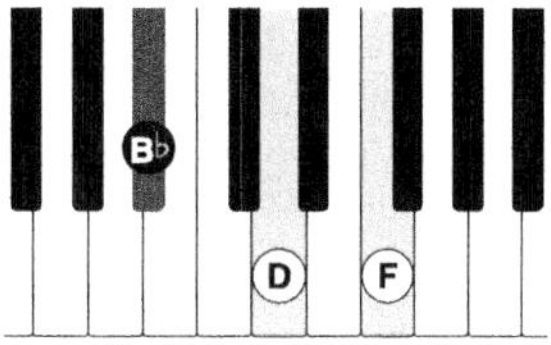

Bb Major Chord

I hope you noticed that 3 of the major chords were made of *all white keys*:

C F G

And I hope you noticed that 3 of the major chords were made of *white keys* on the *outside*, with a *black key* in the *middle*:

D E A

And did you notice that 3 of the major chords were like an Oreo cookie? *Black* on the *outside*, *white* on the *inside*?

Db Eb Ab

That only leaves 3 *major chords*, one of which is *all black*, and one of which is *white, black, black*, and the other the reverse -- *black, white, white*.

Gb (all black) **B** (white, black, black) **Bb** (black, white, white)

And that's it.

Practice playing the first 3 major chords over and over until you can move between them smoothly and quickly. Then practice the next 3 major chords -- then the next 3 -- then the last 3. After you can play them by 3's, practice playing the first 6 without stopping. Then practice the first 9 without stopping. Then finally practice playing all 12 without stopping.

There's no particular virtue, of course, in playing them quickly, except for the fact that it makes you confident you can find them in a hurry when you need them in a song. But you'll find that as your confidence grows, your enjoyment and competence in piano playing with grow commensurately.

With a week's practice you ought to be a pro at all the major chords -- every single one.

In Lesson 5 we'll learn how to stand 'em on their heads, and therefore triple the number of major chords we can play quickly!

All The Minor Chords

If you recall, in Lesson 2 we took an airplane ride over "Chordland" just to get the lay of the land -- the overview of the world of chords.

Then in Lesson 3 we showed you how easy it is to learn ALL the *major chords* (there are 12 of them) and be able to play them in seconds.

Today we are going to cover...

All 12 of the Minor Chords!

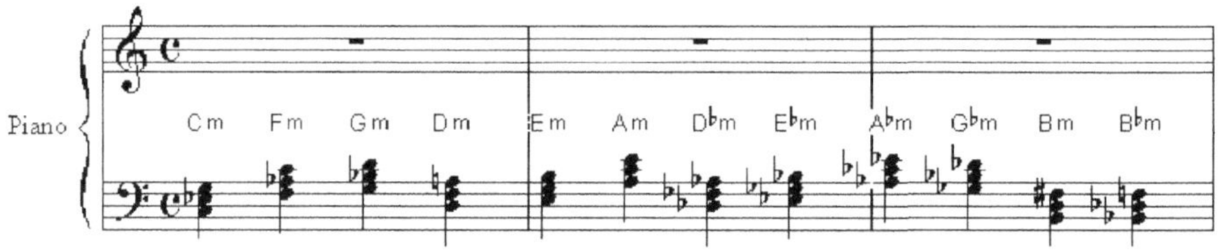

And here's what all the 12 *minor chords* look like on the keyboard:

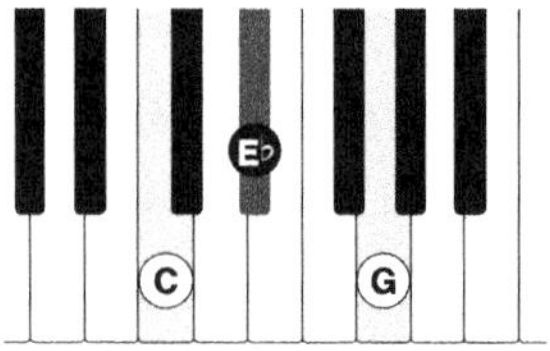

Cm

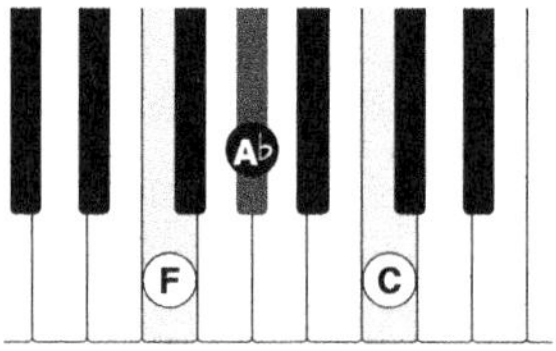

Fm

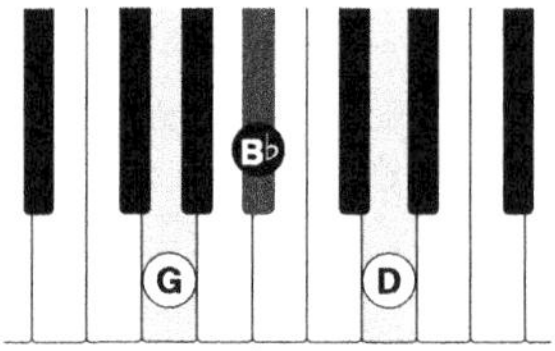

Gm

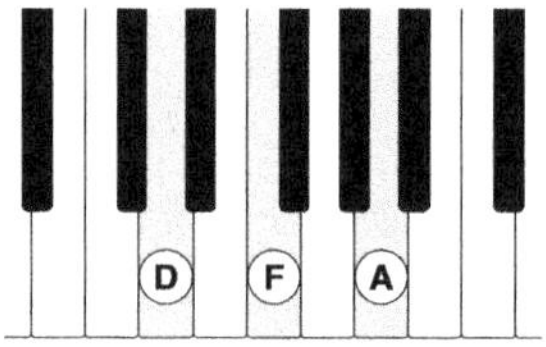

Dm

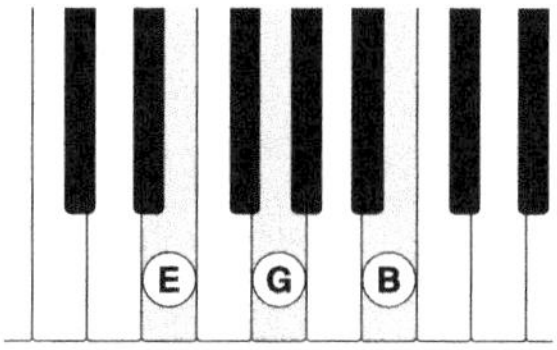

Em

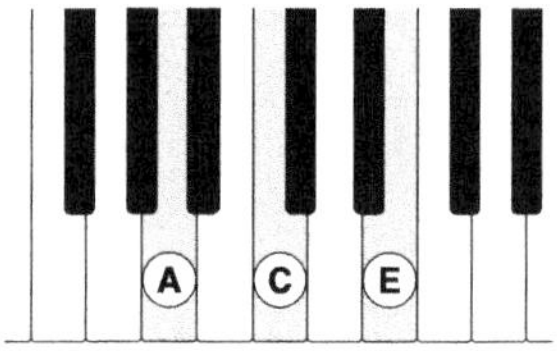

Am

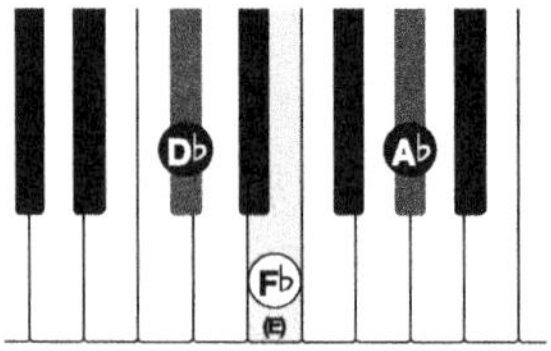

Dbm

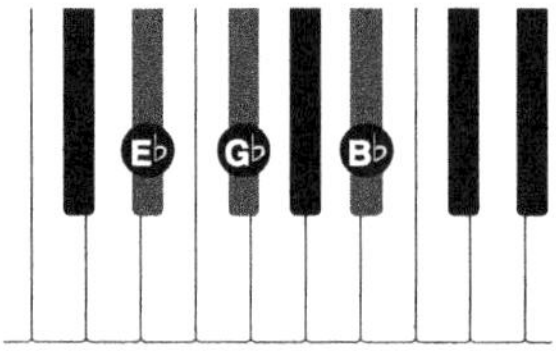

Ebm

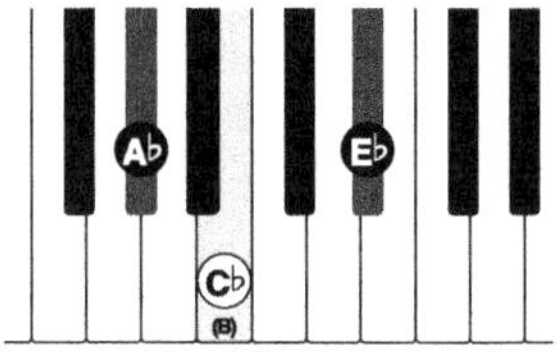

Abm

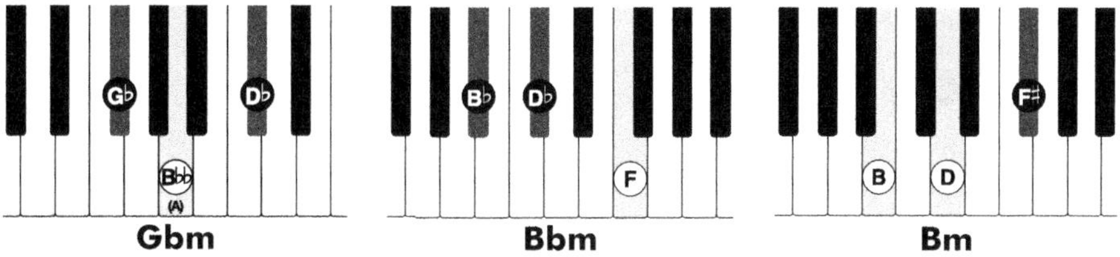

I hope that you noticed that the ONLY DIFFERENCE between *major* and *minor chords* is that the 3rd of the chord is lowered 1/2 step -- that's all. Every major chord is made up of the root, 3rd, and 5th of a major scale, so all you do is lower the 3rd 1/2 step.

And that's it.

Like we did with major chords, practice playing the first 3 chords over and over until you can move between them smoothly and quickly. Then practice the next 3 minor chords -- then the next 3 minor chords-- then the last 3 minor chords. After you can play them by 3's, practice playing the first 6 without stopping. Then practice the first 9 without stopping. Then finally practice playing all 12 minor chords without stopping.

Then play them in major-minor sequence:
In other words, **C major** then **C minor**; **F major** then **F minor**; **G major** then **G minor**, and so on through the 12 chords. Now you have **24** chords under your belt -- **12** major and **12** minor.

There's no particular virtue, of course, in playing them quickly, except for the fact that it makes you confident you can find them in a hurry when you need them in a song. But you'll find that as your confidence grows, your enjoyment and competence in piano playing with grow commensurately.

Now -- to see if you were paying attention, let me give you a little test. One of the minor chords (above) has one key that is mislabeled. Can you find it? The answer is at the bottom of this page*.

That's it for this lesson. With a week's practice you ought to be a pro at all the *major* **and** *minor* chords -- every single one.

In the next lesson we'll learn how to stand 'em on their heads -- all major chords and all minor chords, and therefore triple the number of chords we can play quickly from 24 to 72!

*The **Gbm** chord is mislabeled. The bottom note should be **Gb** – not **Ab**.

Piano Chord Inversions

All The Major & Minor Piano Chords Upside Down

Welcome to Lesson 5. I hope you are enjoying learning about all the chords in the world -- and we're going to cover them ALL before we're done -- you'll know more about chords than 99% of the people in the world -- believe it or not, it's true.

If you recall, in Lesson 1 we learned about the three chords you absolutely, positively CAN'T do without. Then in Lesson 2 we took an airplane ride over "Chordland" just to get the lay of the land -- the overview of the world of chords.

Lesson 3 showed you how easy it is to learn ALL the *major chords* (there are 12 of them) and be able to play them in seconds.

In Lesson 4 you learned how to easily turn *major chords* into *minor chords* just by moving one key one-half step -- by lowering the 3rd of the major chord.

In this lesson we are going to cover chords "*upside down*" -- chords that stand on their head.

If I was strong enough to pick you up and stand you on your head, would you be a different person? Of course not. You would still be you.

And yet many people get all confused when chords are turned upside down. They recognize them when they are in root position, but when you stand 'em on their head....well, it gets kind of fuzzy for folks.

Here's the deal:

Every 3 note chord (called a "triad" -- trio -- tricycle -- meaning "3") can be played in 3 different positions -- *inversions*:

Inversions: Chords Standing On Their Heads

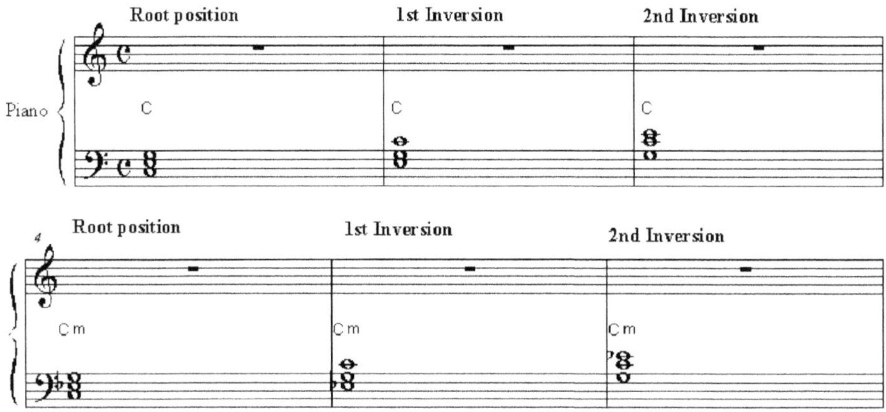

Root position = The name of the chord is the *bottom* note

1st inversion = The name of the chord is the *top* note

2nd inversion = The name of the chord is the *middle* note

And here's what the chord inversions look like on the keyboard:

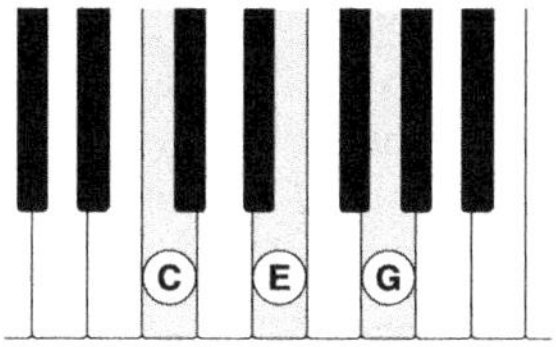

Root Position

Root position (name of chord is *lowest* note)

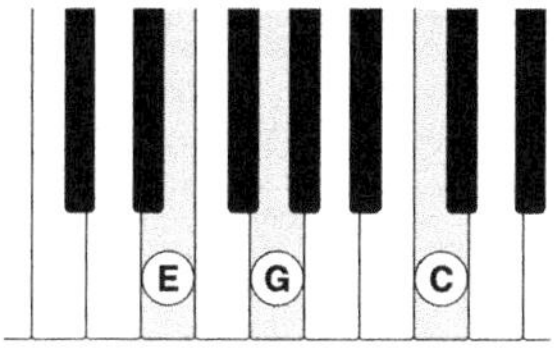

1st Inversion

1st inversion (name of chord is *top* note)

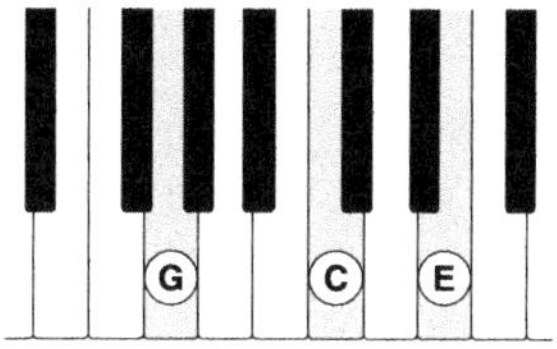

2nd Inversion

2nd inversion (name of chord is the *middle* note)

Now it's up to you. Play each major chord in root position, then 1st inversion, then 2nd inversion. Play each chord up and down the keyboard for at least 2 octaves -- maybe 3 octaves. Play them with your left hand, then play them with your right hand. Then play them hands together.

Go through all 12 major chords, inverting every one. Then go through all the 12 minor chords, inverting each one up and down the keyboard -- hands alone, then hands together.

When you can do that you ought to feel really optimistic about learning chords, because **you've got a great start**. After all, you have gone from:

12 major piano chords *to*

12 minor piano chords *to*

3 inversions of each piano chord

which means you can play **72 piano chords!**

Way to go!

Next lesson we will add 12 more chords to our growing list of chords we can play. We'll take up *diminished triads*, and you'll see how easy they are to learn once you know major and minor chords!

Diminished Piano Triads

The 'Salt' of a Musical Meal

Welcome to Lesson 6. I hope you are enjoying learning about all the chords in the world -- and we're going to cover them ALL before we're done -- you'll know more about chords than 99% of the people in the world -- believe it or not, it's true.

If you recall, in Lesson 1 we learned about the three chords you absolutely, positively CAN'T do without. Then in Lesson 2 we took an airplane ride over "Chordland" just to get the lay of the land -- the overview of the world of chords.

Lesson 3 showed you how easy it is to learn ALL the *major chords* (there are 12 of them) and be able to play them in seconds.

In Lesson 4 you learned how to easily turn *major chords* into *minor chords* just by moving one key one-half step -- by lowering the 3rd of the major chord. Then we learned *inversions* in Lesson 5-- how to stand chords on their head.

In this lesson we are going to *diminished triads*. The formula is real simple:

A **Diminished Triad** = Root - *lowered 3rd* - *lowered 5th*

Here's what they look like on the staff:

Diminished Triads

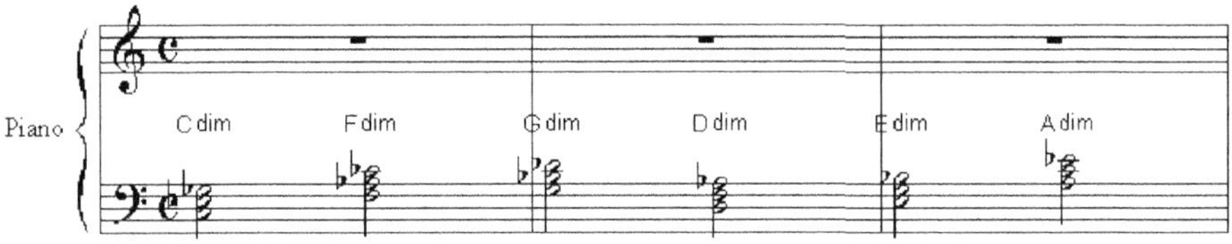

...and I'll let you figure out the other six diminished triads.

And here's what they look like on the keyboard:

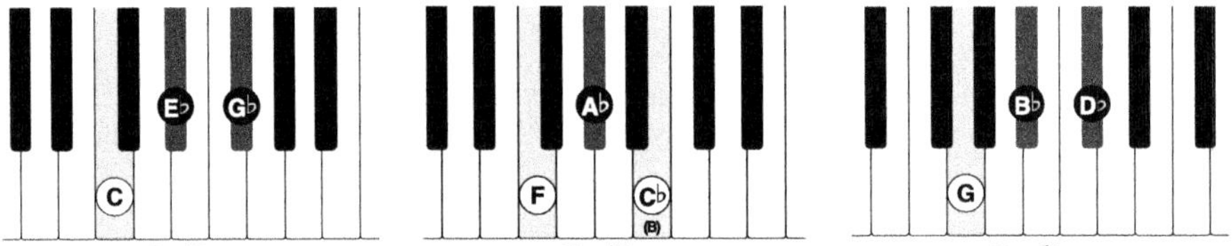

C dim **F dim** **G dim**

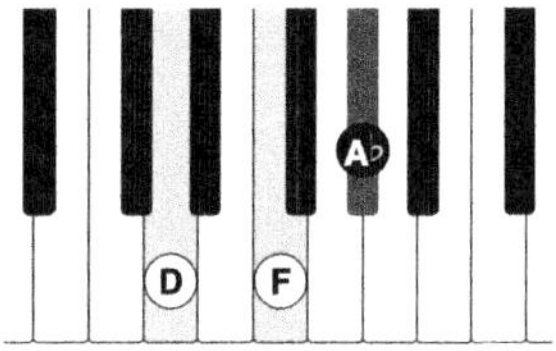

D dim

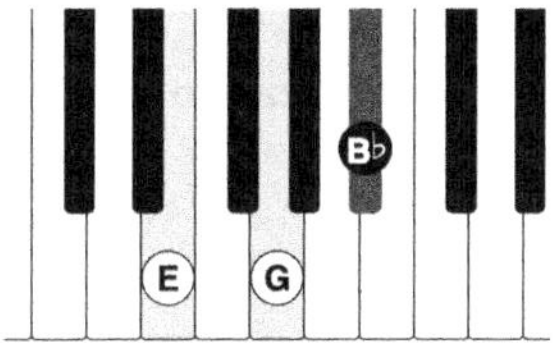

E dim

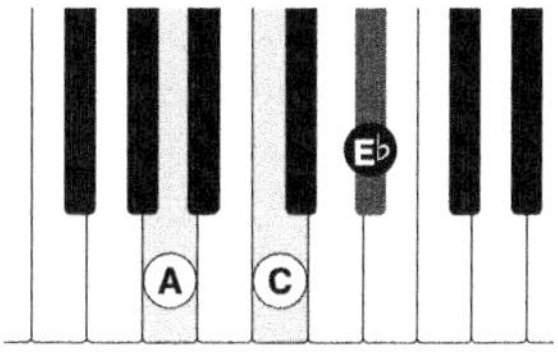

A dim

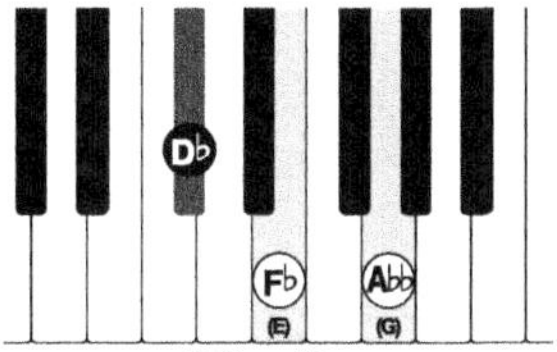

Db dim

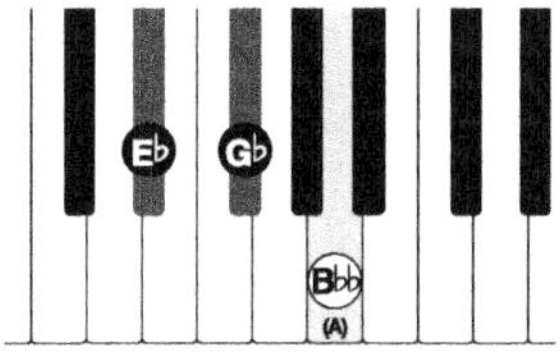

Eb dim

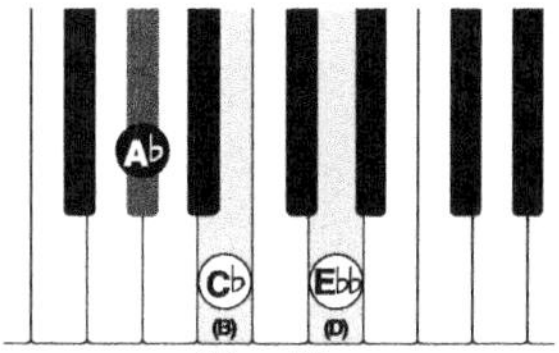

Ab dim

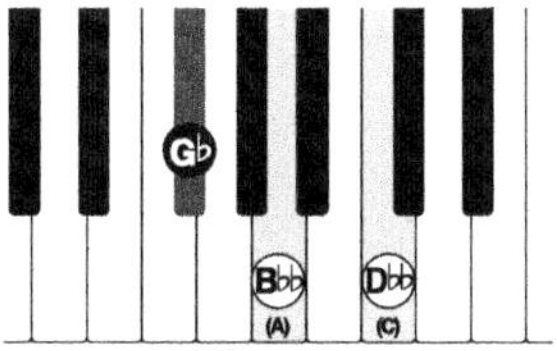

Gb dim

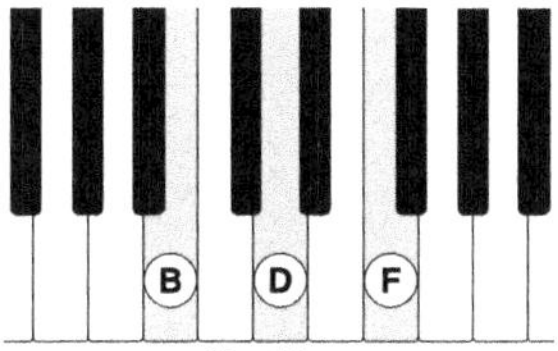

B dim

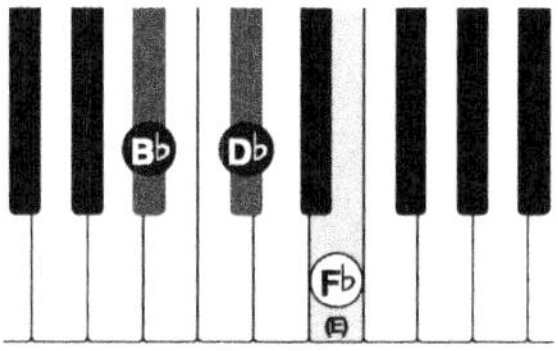

Bb dim

Now it's up to you. Play each diminished triad in root position, then 1st inversion, then 2nd inversion. Play each chord up and down the keyboard for at least 2 octaves -- maybe 3 octaves. Play them with your left hand, then play them with your right hand. Then play them hands together.

Go through all 12 major chords, inverting every one. Then go through all the 12 minor chords, inverting each one up and down the keyboard -- hands alone, then hands together. Finally, go through all 12 diminished chords, inverting each one up and down the keyboard -- each hand alone, then together. Then skip around from major to minor to diminished, etc.

When you can do that you ought to feel **really optimistic about learning chords**, because you've got a great start. After all, you have gone from:

12 major piano chords *to*

12 minor piano chords *to*

12 diminished piano chords *and*

3 inversions of each piano chord

which means you can play **108 piano chords!**

Way to go!

Next lesson we will add 12 more chords to our growing list of chords we can play. We'll take up *augmented triads* -- they are like the "pepper" of a musical meal, and you'll see how easy they are to learn once you know major and minor and diminished chords!

Augmented Piano Triads

The 'Pepper' of a Musical Meal

Welcome to Lesson 7. I hope you are enjoying learning about all the chords in the world -- and we're going to cover them ALL before we're done -- you'll know more about chords than 99% of the people in the world -- believe it or not, it's true.

If you recall, in Lesson 1 we learned about the three chords you absolutely, positively CAN'T do without. Then in Lesson 2 we took an airplane ride over "Chordland" just to get the lay of the land -- the overview of the world of chords.

Lesson 3 showed you how easy it is to learn ALL the *major chords* (there are 12 of them) and be able to play them in seconds. In Lesson 4 you learned how to easily turn *major chords* into *minor chords* just by moving one key one-half step -- by lowering the 3rd of the major chord.

Then we learned *inversions* in Lesson 5 -- how to stand chords on their head, and we learned *diminished triads* in Lesson 6-- just by lowering the 3rd and the 5th of a major chord 1/2 step.

In this lesson we are going to learn *augmented chords*. They are the "pepper" of a musical meal, much like the diminished triads were the "salt" of a musical meal.

You wouldn't make a meal out of them, but you use them as seasoning -- to liven up your music.

The formula is real simple:

An **Augmented Triad** = Root - 3rd - *raised 5th*

Here's what they look like on the staff:

Augmented Triads

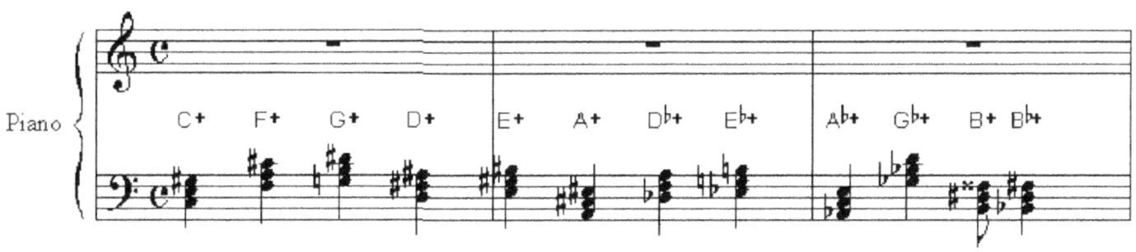

(The symbol for an augmented chord is a "+" sign)

And here's what they look like on the keyboard:

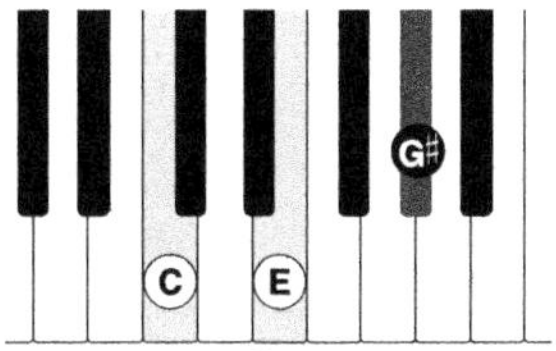

C+

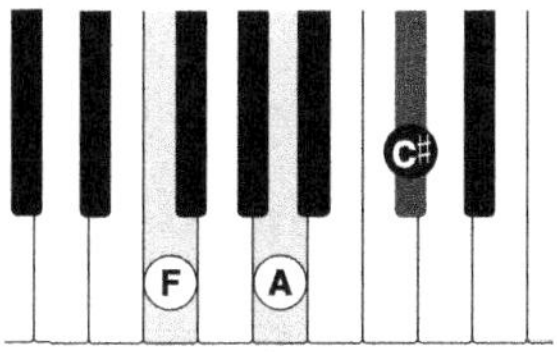

F+

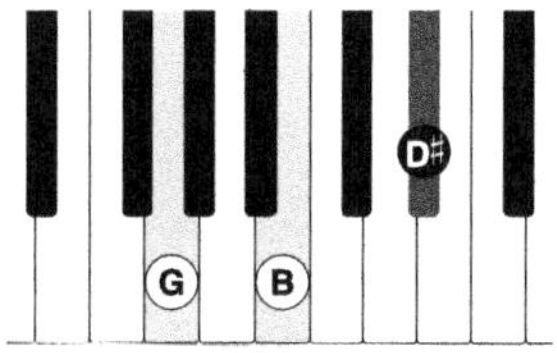

G+

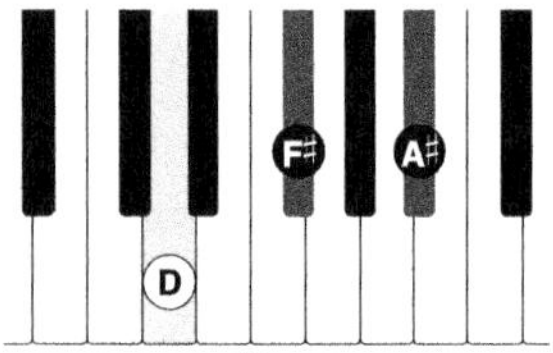

D+

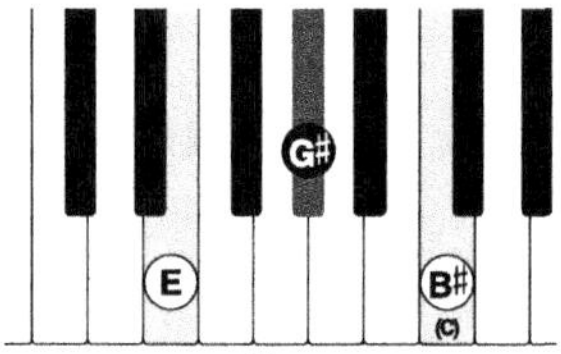

E+

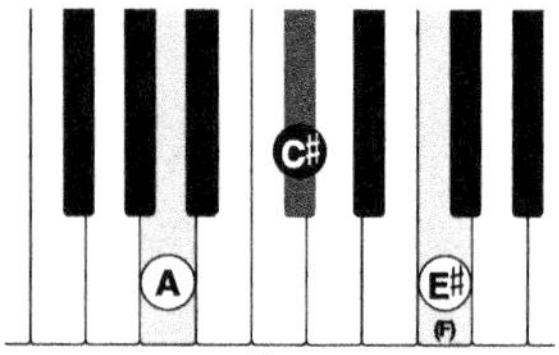

A+

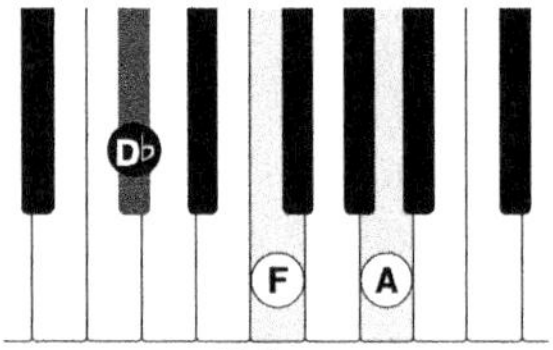

Db+

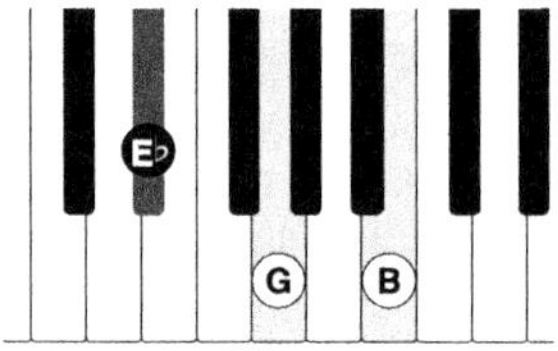

Eb+

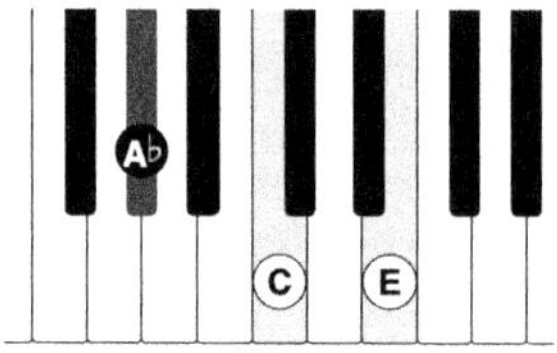

Ab+

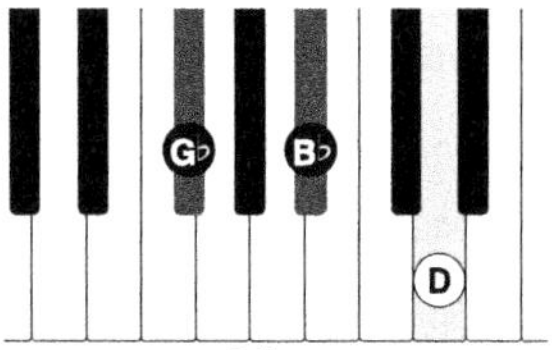

Gb+

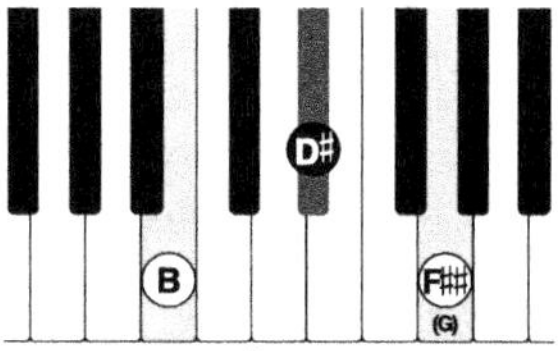

B+

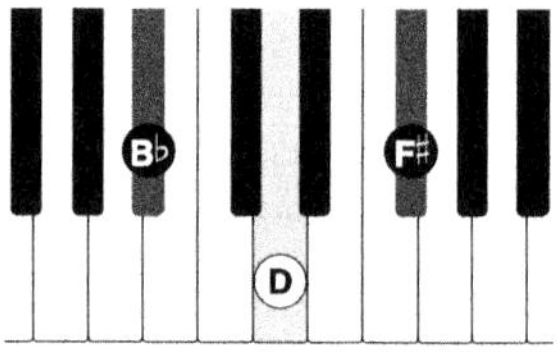

Bb+

Now it's up to you. Play each augmented triad in root position, then 1st inversion, then 2nd inversion. Play each chord up and down the keyboard for at least 2 octaves -- maybe 3 octaves. Play them with your left hand, then play them with your right hand. Then play them hands together.

Go through all 12 major chords, inverting every one. Then go through all the 12 minor chords, inverting each one up and down the keyboard -- hands alone, then hands together. Then go through all 12 diminished chords, inverting each one up and down the keyboard -- each hand alone, then together. Then play the 12 augmented chords, up and down the keyboard. Then skip around from major to minor to diminished to augmented, etc.

When you can do that you ought to feel **really, really, really optimistic about learning chords**, because you've got a great start. After all, you have gone from:

12 major piano chords *to*

12 minor piano chords *to*

12 diminished piano chords *to*

12 augmented piano chords *and*

3 inversions of each piano chord

which means you can play **144 piano chords!**

That's **12 dozen** -- ***a gross of piano chords***!

That's more than most people learn in their *entire life* -- and you've learned them in **7 lessons**!

Yea!

Way to go!

In the next lesson we will add 24 more chords to our growing list of chords we can play. Now that we have covered all the triads (3 note chords), we'll take up *6th chords* -- they are extensions of the basic major and minor chords.

All The Major 6th Piano Chords

The first of the extended chords group

Welcome to Lesson 8. I hope you are enjoying learning about all the chords in the world -- and we're going to cover them ALL before we're done -- you'll know more about chords than 99% of the people in the world -- believe it or not, it's true.

If you recall, in Lesson 1 the first week we learned about the three chords you absolutely, positively CAN'T do without. Then in Lesson 2 we took an airplane ride over "Chordland" just to get the lay of the land -- the overview of the world of chords.

Lesson 3 showed you how easy it is to learn ALL the *major chords* (there are 12 of them) and be able to play them in seconds. In Lesson 4 you learned how to easily turn *major chords* into *minor chords* just by moving one key one-half step -- by lowering the 3rd of the major chord.

Then we learned *inversions* in Lesson 5 -- how to stand chords on their head, and we learned *diminished triads* in Lesson 6 -- just by lowering the 3rd and the 5th of a major chord 1/2 step.

And in Lesson 7, we took up *augmented triads* -- formed by simply raising the 5th of a major triad.

In this lesson we are going to learn *major 6th chords*. They are 4-note chords -- the root, 3rd, 5th -- just like a *major chord*, but you also add the *6th degree* of the scale to the major triad.

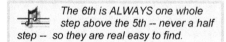

The 6th is ALWAYS one whole step above the 5th -- never a half step -- so they are real easy to find.

So here is the formula:

A **Major 6th Chord** = Root - 3rd - 5th - *6th*

Here's what *major 6th* piano chords look like on the staff:

All the 6th Chords

(Remember that accidentals carry over in each measure!)

And here's what they look like when played in root position: (They appear in the same order as the notation above -- besides, you should be able to form them by now, since all there is to it is to add the 6th note of the scale to the major chord!)

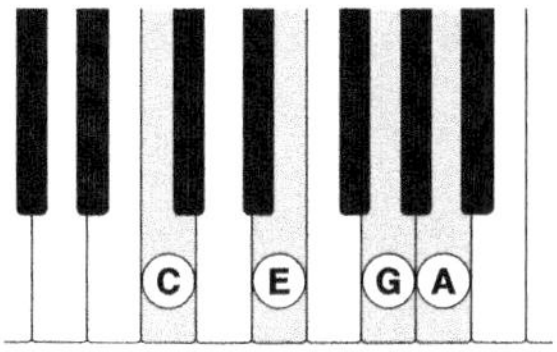

C6

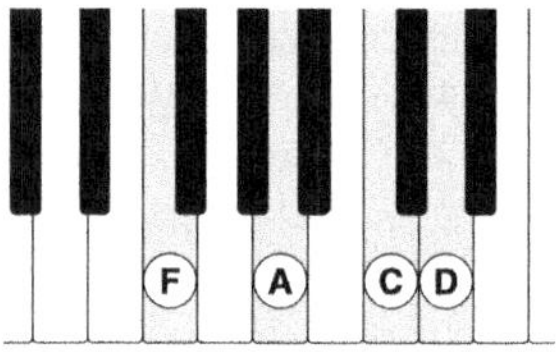

F6

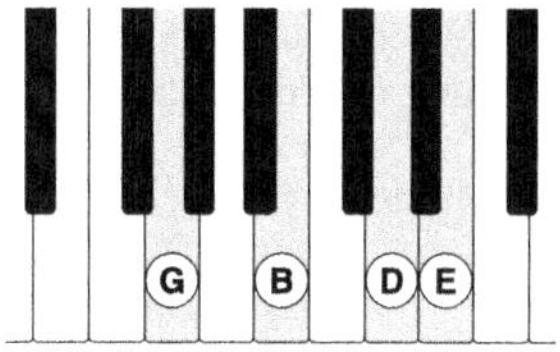

G6

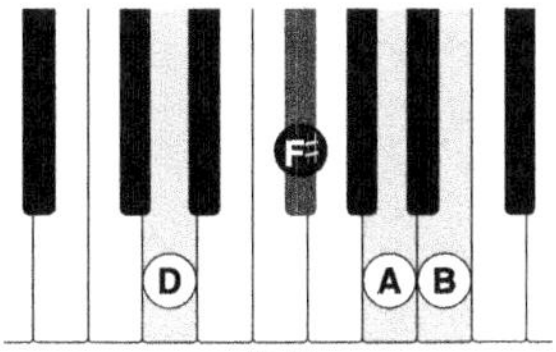

D6

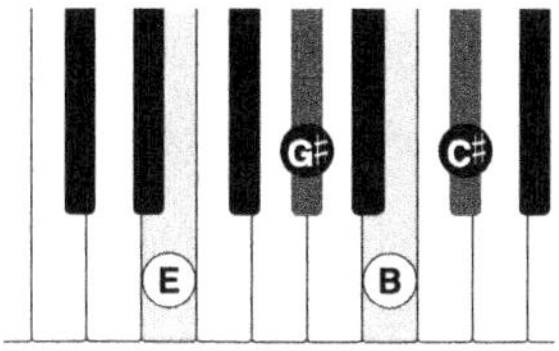

E6

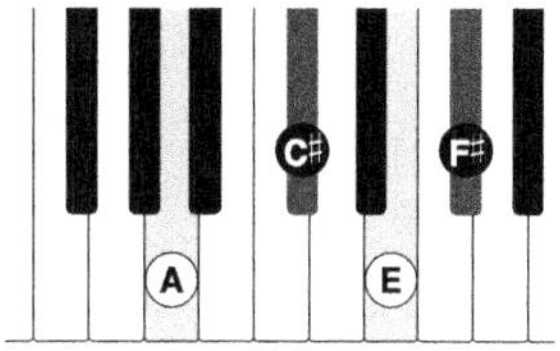

A6

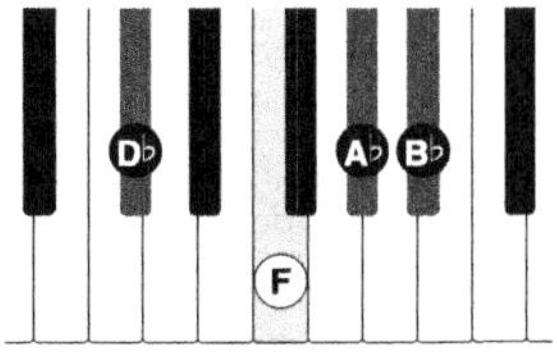

Db6

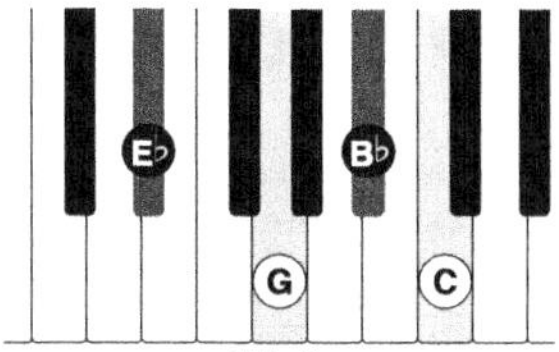

Eb6

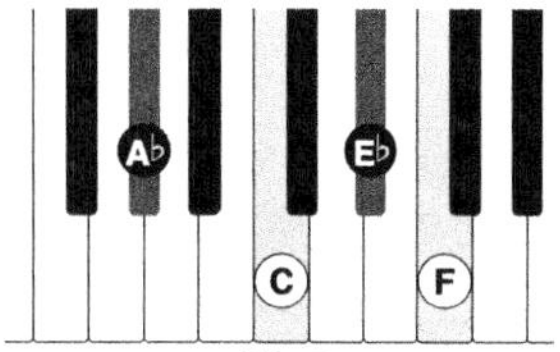

Ab6

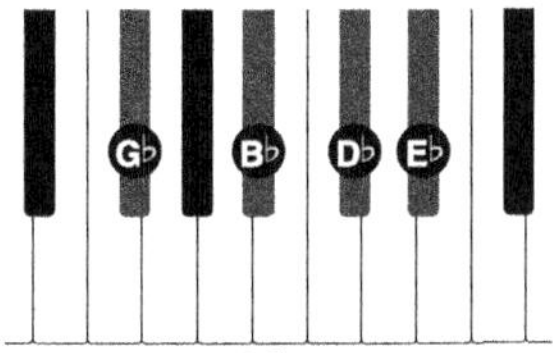

Gb6

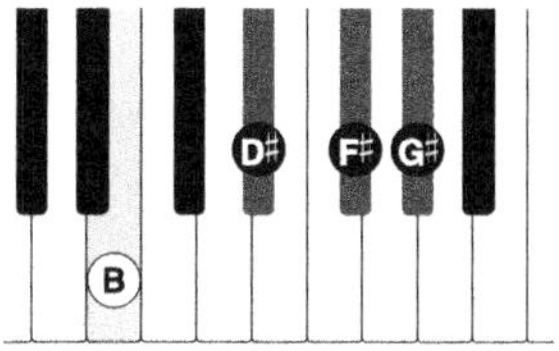

B6

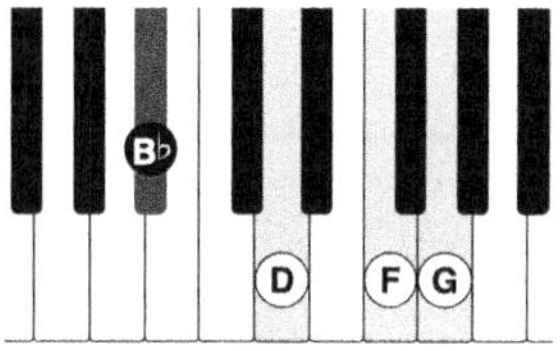

Bb6

Now it's up to you. Play each augmented triad in root position, then 1st inversion, then 2nd inversion. Play each chord up and down the keyboard for at least 2 octaves -- maybe 3 octaves. Play them with your left hand, then play them with your right hand. Then play them hands together.

Go through all 12 major chords, inverting every one. Then go through all the 12 minor chords, inverting each one up and down the keyboard -- hands alone, then hands together. Then go through all 12 diminished chords, inverting each one up and down the keyboard -- each hand alone, then together. Then play the 12 augmented chords, up and down the keyboard. Then skip around from major to minor to diminished to augmented, etc.

Now add major 6th chords to your repertoire of chords. They are shown in root position above, but you know that you can turn them upside down 'till the cows come home -- invert them -- so go to it!

When you can do that you ought to feel **really, really, really, really optimistic about learning chords**, because you're on your way! After all, you have gone from:

12 major piano chords *to*

12 minor piano chords *to*

12 diminished piano chords *to*

12 augmented piano chords *and*

12 major 6th piano chords *and*

inversions of each piano chord

which means you can now play **192 piano chords!**

Good for you!

Next lesson we will add 12 more chords to our growing list of chords we can play by adding *minor 6th chords* to our stash. (Actually **48** more chords, since each 4-note chord such as a minor 6th can be inverted 4 ways -- root position, 1st inversion, 2nd inversion, and 3rd inversion.

All The Minor 6th Piano Chords

Another extended piano chord you need to know!

Welcome to Lesson 9. I hope you are enjoying learning about all the chords in the world -- and we're going to cover them ALL before we're done -- you'll know more about chords than 99% of the people in the world -- believe it or not, it's true.

If you recall, in Lesson 1 we learned about the three chords you absolutely, positively CAN'T do without. Then in Lesson 2 we took an airplane ride over "Chordland" just to get the lay of the land -- the overview of the world of chords.

Lesson 3 showed you how easy it is to learn ALL the *major chords* (there are 12 of them) and be able to play them in seconds. In Lesson 4 you learned how to easily turn *major chords* into *minor chords* just by moving one key one-half step -- by lowering the 3rd of the major chord.

Then we learned *inversions* in Lesson 5-- how to stand chords on their head, and we learned *diminished triads* in Lesson 6-- just by lowering the 3rd and the 5th of a major chord 1/2 step.

With Lesson 7 we took up *augmented triads* -- formed by simply raising the 5th of a major triad, and we learned about *major 6th chords* in Lesson 8. They are 4-note chords -- the root, 3rd, 5th -- just like a major chord, but you also add the 6th degree of the scale to the major triad.

In this lesson, we will change those *major 6th chords* into *minor 6th chords* just by altering the 3rd 1/2 step -- in other words, a minor triad with a 6th on top.

So here is the formula for a minor 6th chord:

A **Minor 6th Piano Chord** = Root - flat3rd - 5th - 6th

Here's what *Minor 6th piano chords* look like on the staff:

All the Minor 6th Chords

(Remember that accidentals carry over in each measure!)

And here's what they look like on the piano keyboard when played in root position:

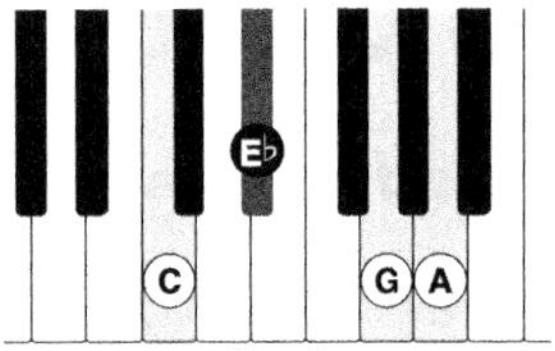

Cm6

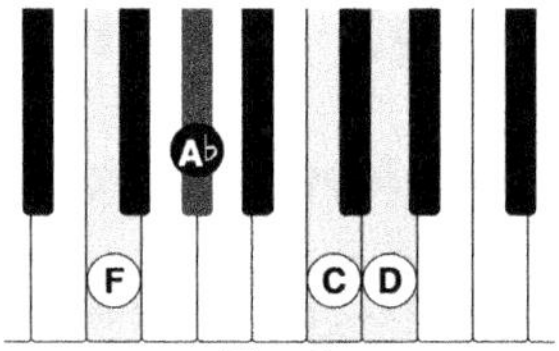

Fm6

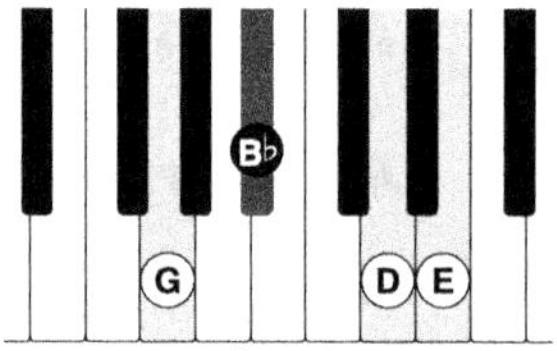

Gm6

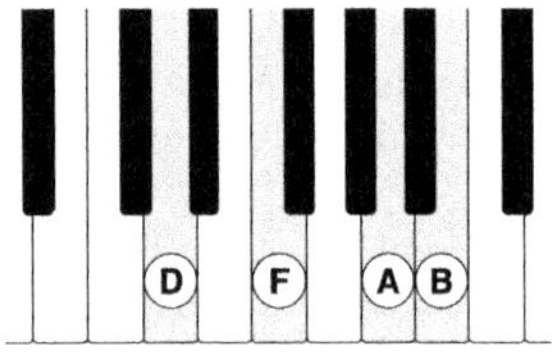

Dm6

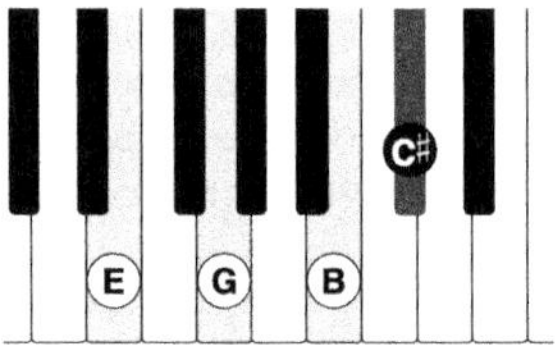

Em6

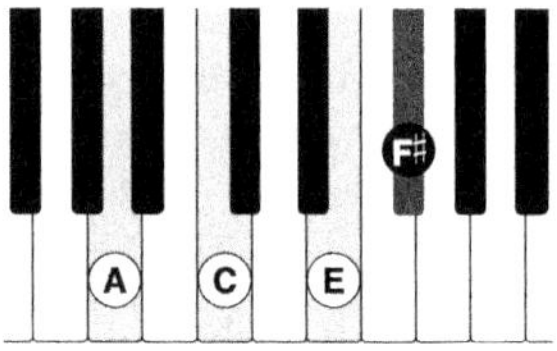

Am6

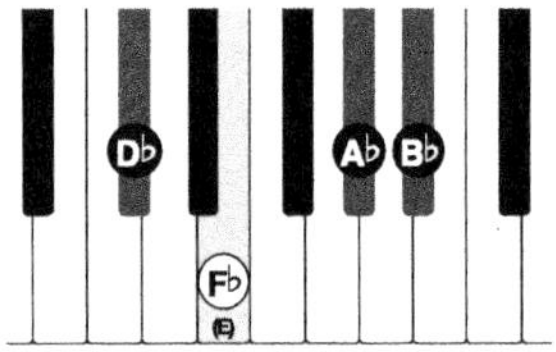

Dbm6

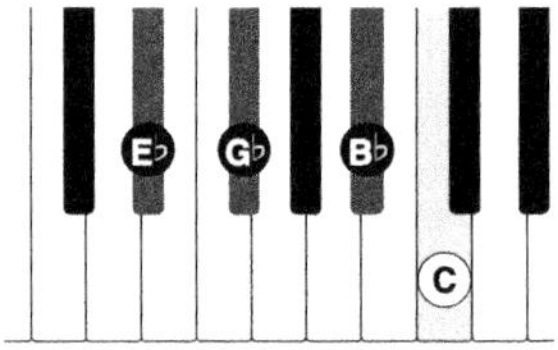

Ebm6

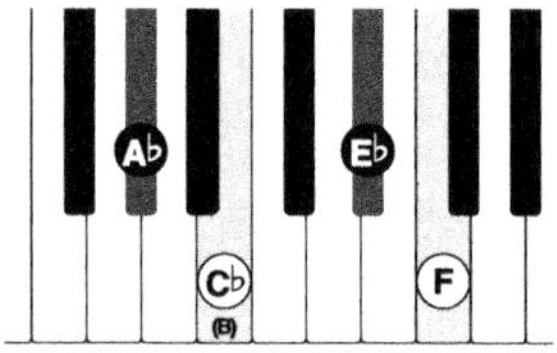

Abm6

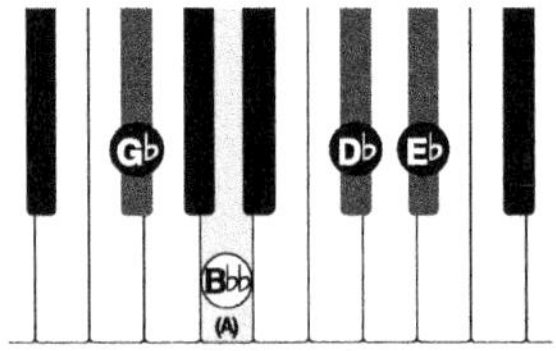

Gbm6

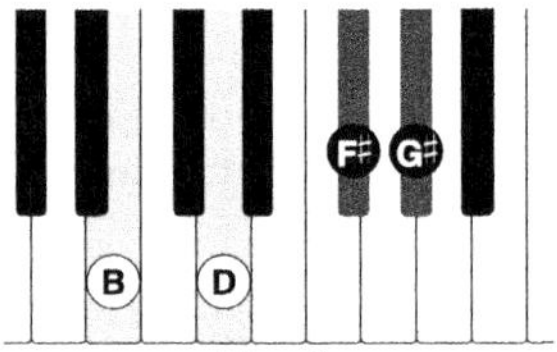

Bm6

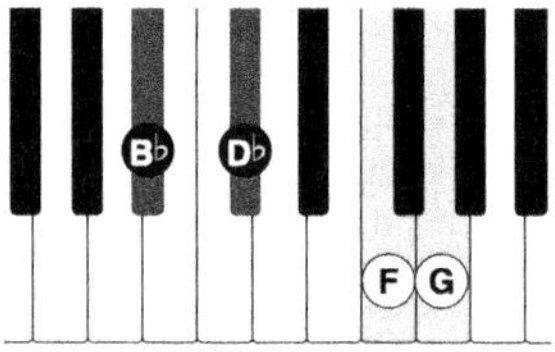

Bbm6

As usual, now it's up to you. Play each minor 6th chord in root position, then 1st inversion, then 2nd inversion, then in 3rd inversion (the 6th will be the lowest note of the chord) Play each chord up and down the keyboard for at least 2 octaves -- maybe 3 octaves. Play them with your left hand, then play them with your right hand. Then play them hands together.

Go through all 12 major chords, inverting every one. Then go through all the 12 minor chords, inverting each one up and down the keyboard -- hands alone, then hands together. Then go through all 12 diminished chords, inverting each one up and down the keyboard -- each hand alone, then together. Then play the 12 augmented chords, up and down the keyboard. Then skip around from major to minor to diminished to augmented, etc. Next, add major 6th chords.

Now add minor 6th chords to your repertoire of chords. They are shown in root position above, but you know that you can turn them upside down 'till the cows come home -- invert them -- so go to it!

Do you feel like you're getting a handle on chords yet? You ought to -- I know we're going slowly, but chords are *SO important* that you **absolutely MUST master them** if you are ever going to play the piano like you hope to!

So here's our revised chord scorecard:

12 major piano chords *to*

12 minor piano chords *to*

12 diminished piano chords *to*

12 augmented piano chords *and*

12 major 6th piano chords *and*

12 minor 6th piano chords *and*

inversions of each piano chords

which means you can now play **240 piano chords!**

Excellent!

Next lesson we will add 12 more chords to our growing list of chords we can play by adding *7th chords* to our stash. (Actually **48** more chords, since each 4-note chord such as a 7th can be inverted 4 ways -- root position, 1st inversion, 2nd inversion, and 3rd inversion.)

All The 7th Piano Chords

One of the most valuable chord types you'll ever learn...

> *Welcome to Lesson 10.. I hope you are enjoying learning about all the chords in the world -- and we're going to cover them ALL before we're done -- you'll know more about chords than 99% of the people in the world -- believe it or not, it's true.*

If you recall, in Lesson 1 we learned about the three chords you absolutely, positively CAN'T do without. Then in Lesson 2 we took an airplane ride over "Chordland" just to get the lay of the land -- the overview of the world of chords.

Lesson 3 showed you how easy it is to learn ALL the *major chords* (there are 12 of them) and be able to play them in seconds. In Lesson 4 you learned how to easily turn *major chords* into *minor chords* just by moving one key one-half step -- by lowering the 3rd of the major chord.

Then we learned *inversions* in Lesson 5-- how to stand chords on their head, and we learned *diminished triads* in Lesson 6-- just by lowering the 3rd and the 5th of a major chord 1/2 step.

With Lesson 7 we took up *augmented triads* -- formed by simply raising the 5th of a major triad, we learned about *major 6th chords* in Lesson 8. They are 4-note chords -- the root, 3rd, 5th -- just like a major chord, but you also add the 6th degree of the scale to the major triad.

Then, in Lesson 9 we changed those *major 6th chords* into *minor 6th chords* just by altering the 3rd 1/2 step -- in other words, a minor triad with a 6th on top.

In this lesson, we're going to take up *7th chords* -- very important chords, because they move you from one tonal base to another tonal base. In other words, when we move from the **C** chord to the **F** chord, we often use **C7** between the two as a "connector."

> *Actually, there are two types of 7th chords -- a 7th, which we're considering today, and a major 7th, which we will take up in Lesson 11.*

To form a *7th chord*, just find the 7th note of the scale and lower it 1/2 step. (Next lesson we'll take up the "*Major 7th*" chord, which uses the scale 7th.) But with a plain *7th chord*, we lower the 7th 1/2 step. So here is the formula for a *7th chord*:

A **7th Piano Chord** = Root - 3rd - 5th - flat7th

Just add the lowered 7th note of the scale -- *not the 7th* -- **the lowered 7th** -- to the major triad.

Here's what *7th piano chords* look like on the staff:

7th Chords

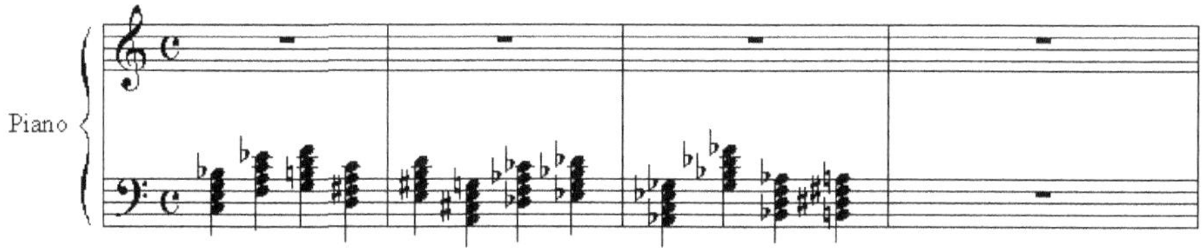

(Remember that accidentals carry over in each measure!)

And here's what they look like when played with the left hand:

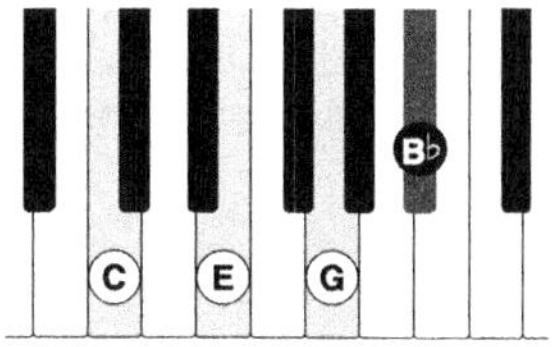

C7

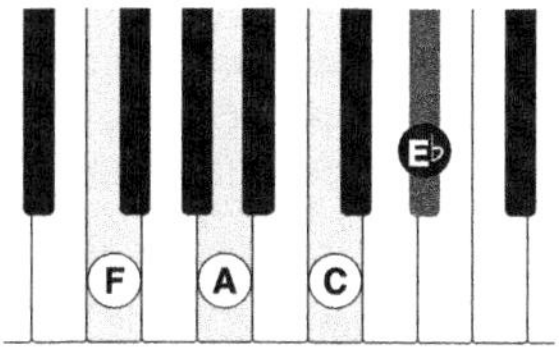

F7

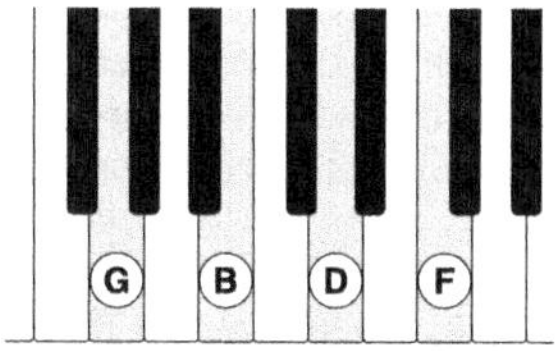

G7

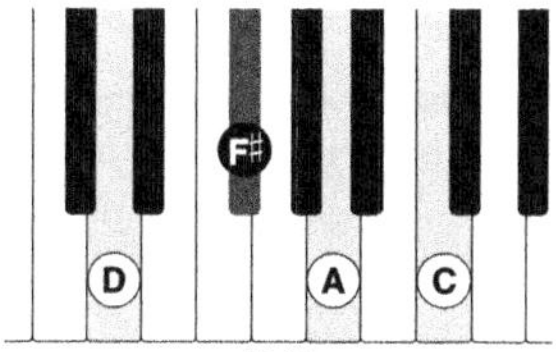

D7

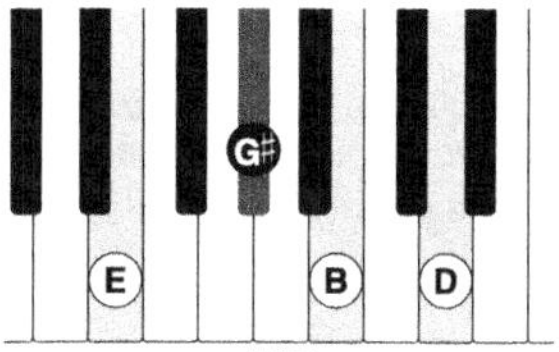

E7

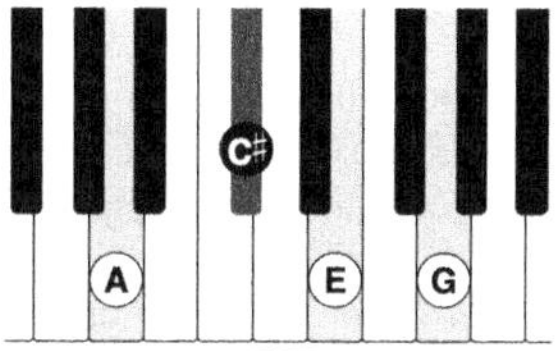

A7

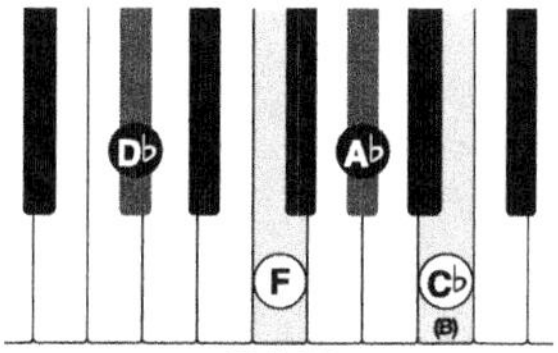

Db7

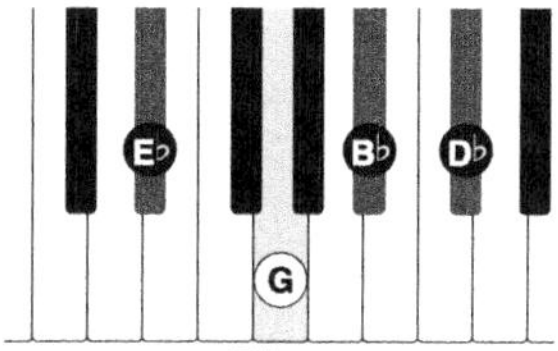

Eb7

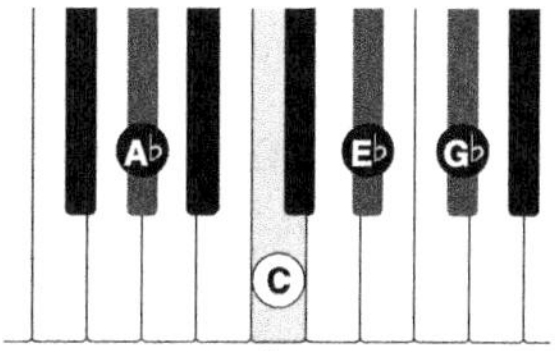

Ab7

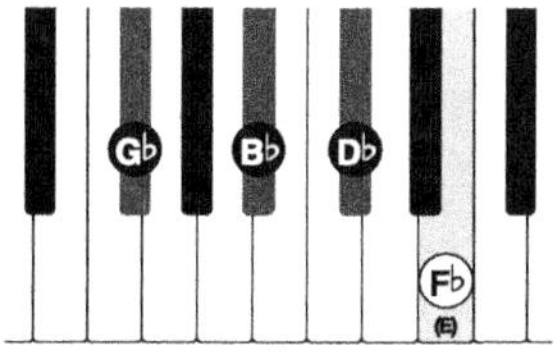

Gb7

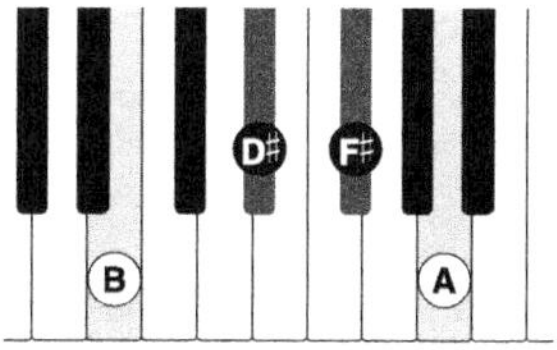

B7

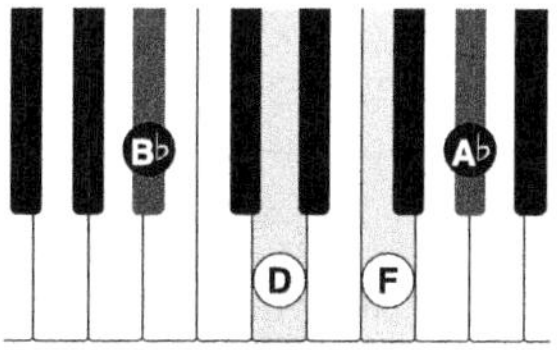

Bb7

(They appear in the same order as before:)

C7 F7 G7 D7 E7 A7 Db7 Eb7 Ab7 Gb7 B7 Bb7

7th chords want to move up a perfect 4th -- they don't have to, but that is their tendency. So if you encounter a **G7** chord, what is the next likely chord? Sure -- a **C** chord. Why? Because it's a *4th higher* than **G**. If you encountered an **Eb7** chord, what is the most likely chord to follow it? Right. **Ab**. Why? Because **Ab** is a *4th above* **Eb**.

Just knowing that gives you a tiny idea of how much you can gain from knowing chord progressions, which we will take up as soon as we get through learning all the chords.

As usual, now it's up to you. Play each 7th chord in root position, then 1st inversion, then 2nd inversion, then in 3rd inversion (the 7th will be the lowest note of the chord) Play each chord up and down the keyboard for at least 2 octaves -- maybe 3 octaves. Play them with your left hand, then play them with your right hand. Then play them hands together.

Go through all 12 major chords, inverting every one. Then go through all the 12 minor chords, inverting each one up and down the keyboard -- hands alone, then hands together. Then go through all 12 diminished chords, inverting each one up and down the keyboard -- each hand alone, then together. Then play the 12 augmented chords, up and down the keyboard. Then skip around from major to minor to diminished to augmented, etc.

Then add major 6th and minor 6th chords to your repertoire of chords. You know that you can turn them upside down 'till the cows come home -- invert them -- so go to it!

And then add 7th chords and their inversions.

Do you feel like you're getting a handle on chords yet? You ought to -- I know we're going slowly, but chords are *SO important* that you **absolutely MUST master them** if you are ever going to play the piano like you hope to!

So here's our revised chord scorecard:

12 major piano chords *to*

12 minor piano chords *to*

12 diminished piano chords *to*

12 augmented piano chords *and*

12 major 6th piano chords *and*

12 minor 6th piano chords *and*

now **twelve** 7th piano chords (that makes **96** chords!) *and*

3 or 4 inversions of each piano chord

which means you can now play **over 300 piano chords!**

Yea! Gimme a High Five!

Next lesson we will add 12 more chords to our growing list of chords we can play by adding *major 7th chords* to our stash. (Actually **48** more chords, since each 4-note chord such as a 7th can be inverted 4 ways -- root position, 1st inversion, 2nd inversion, and 3rd inversion.)

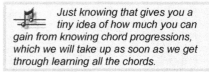

All The Major 7th Chords

The symbol for Major 7th chords is "maj7"

Welcome to Lesson 11. I hope you are enjoying learning about all the chords in the world -- and we're going to cover them ALL before we're done -- you'll know more about chords than 99% of the people in the world -- believe it or not, it's true.

Last time we covered 7th chords. Today we're going to learn *major 7th chords* -- only 1/2 step different, but a HUGE difference in the sound and how they are used. 7th chords are extremely common -- used in all kinds of music. Major 7th chords are less common, and are generally used as "color chords" to create a certain sound, a certain mood.

To form a *major 7th chord*, simply add the 7th degree of the scale to the major triad. For example, you know that the **C** major triad is **C - E - G**. You also know that the **C** scale has 8 notes, the 7th of which is **B**. So by adding **B** to the **C** major triad, we create a **Cmaj7** chord:

A **Major 7th Chord** = Root - 3rd - 5th - 7th

Just add the 7th note of the scale to the major triad.

Here's what *Major 7th chords* look like on the staff:

All 12 Major 7th Chords

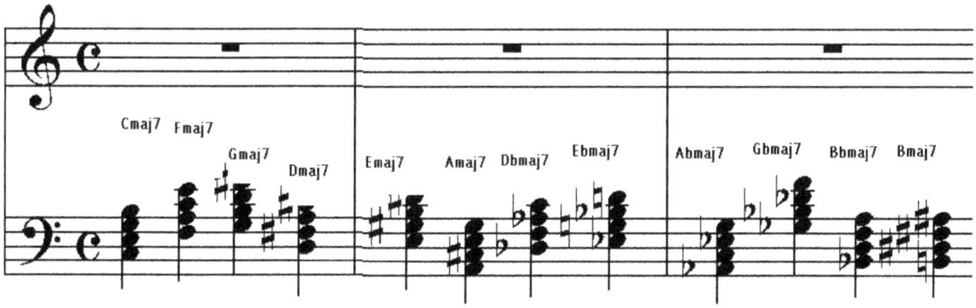

(Remember that accidentals carry over in the same measure!)

And here's what they look like when played with your left hand on the keyboard:

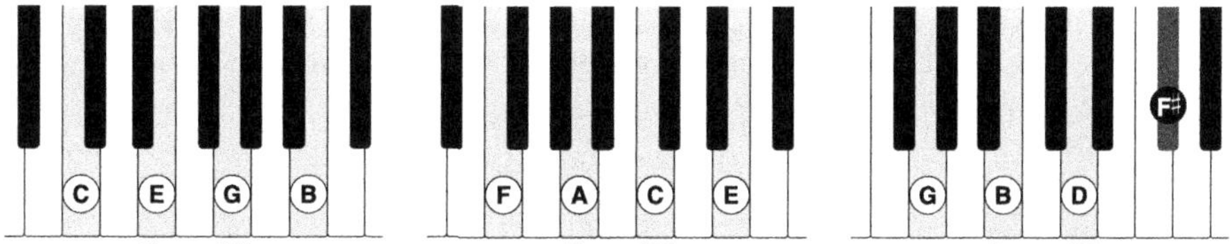

Cmaj7 **Fmaj7** **Gmaj7**

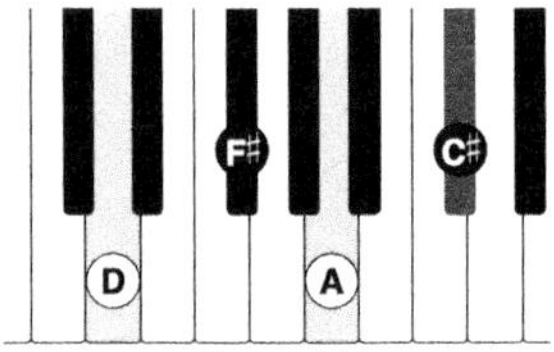

Dmaj7

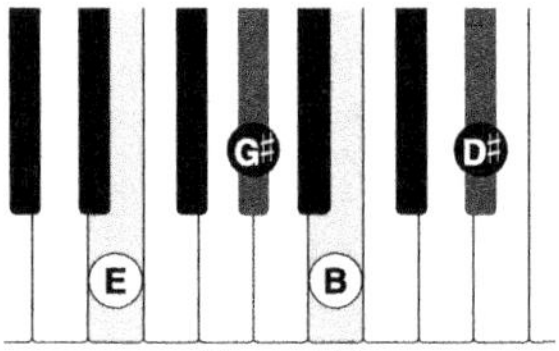

Emaj7

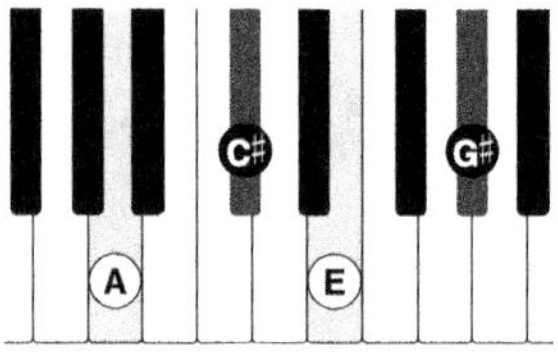

Amaj7

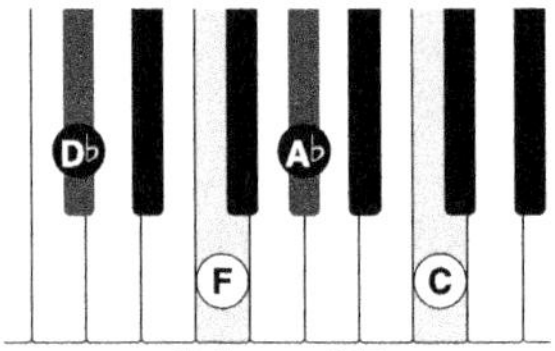

Dbmaj7

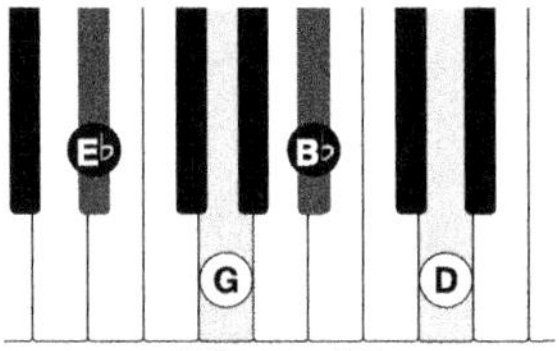

Ebmaj7

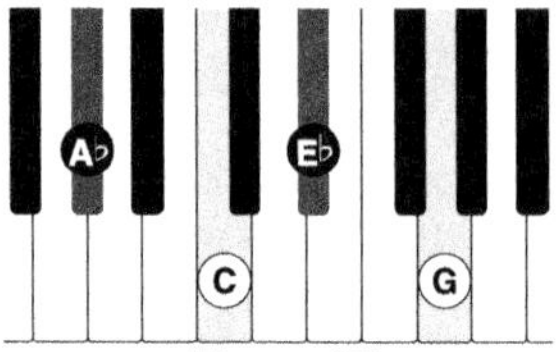

Abmaj7

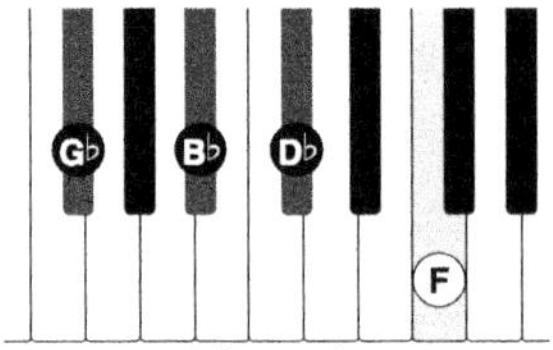

Gbmaj7

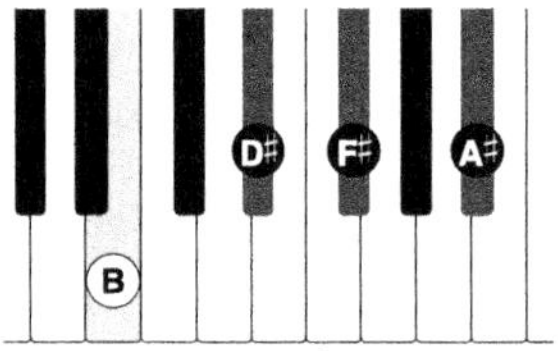

Bmaj7

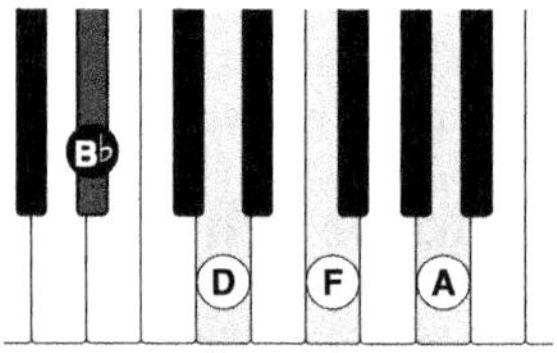

Bbmaj7

As usual, now it's up to you. Play each *maj7th chord* in root position, then 1st inversion, then 2nd inversion, then in 3rd inversion (the maj7th will be the lowest note of the chord) Play each chord up and down the keyboard for at least 2 octaves -- maybe 3 octaves. Play them with your left hand, then play them with your right hand. Then play them hands together.

Go through all 12 major chords, inverting every one. Then go through all the 12 minor chords, inverting each one up and down the keyboard -- hands alone, then hands together. Then go through all 12 diminished chords, inverting each one up and down the keyboard -- each hand alone, then together. Then play the 12 augmented chords, up and down the keyboard. Then skip around from major to minor to diminished to augmented, etc.

Then add major 6th and minor 6th chords to your repertoire of chords. You know that you can turn them upside down 'till the cows come home -- invert them -- so go to it!

And then add 7th chords and their inversions....and finally, add the maj7th chords we've learned in this lesson.

Do you feel like you're getting a handle on chords yet? You ought to -- I know we're going slowly, but chords are *SO important* that you **absolutely MUST master them** if you are ever going to play the piano like you hope to!

So here's our revised chord scorecard:

12 major chords *to*

12 minor chords *to*

12 diminished chords *to*

12 augmented chords *and*

12 major 6th chords *and*

12 minor 6th chords *and*

twelve 7th chords *and*

twelve maj7th chords *and*

3 or 4 inversions of each

which means you can now play **over 350 chords!**

Way to go!

Next lesson we will add 12 more chords to our growing list of chords we can play by adding *9th chords* to our stash. (Actually **48** more chords, since each 4-note chord such as a 9th can be inverted 4 ways -- root position, 1st inversion, 2nd inversion, and 3rd inversion - and if your hand is big enough -- mine isn't -- 4th inversion.)

All The 9th Piano Chords

Welcome to Lesson 12. I hope you are enjoying learning about all the chords in the world -- and we're going to cover them ALL before we're done -- you'll know more about piano chords than 99% of the people in the world -- believe it or not, it's true.

Last lesson we covered maj7th chords. That was the last of the piano chords you can play without doing some fancy maneuvering. Today we're going to learn *9th chords*, and from now on we will be inverting the chords and using a 2-step process to play the piano chords.

A *9th chord* is made up of a root, a 3rd, a 5th, a 7th (not the maj7th -- just the 7th) plus the 9th note of the scale, which of course is the same as the 2nd note of the scale, but an octave higher.

Why don't we call it a "2nd", then, instead of a 9th? Because the chord has a 7th under the 9th, whereas a 2nd wouldn't have a 7th under it.

So:

A **9th Piano Chord** = Root - 3rd - 5th - 7th - *9th*

Add the 9th note of the scale to the 4-note 7th chord -- therefore we have a *5-note* piano chord.

What's the problem with a 5 note piano chord? Nothing, except if your hand is small like mine. I can't reach all 5 keys, so I had to come up with another way to position the chord on the keyboard.

And even if your hand is big enough to reach a 9th, you won't have enough fingers to play an 11th or 13th! So you have to come up with a way to play those humungous chords, and this is the best way I've found -- though not the only way.

What we do is this:

Get your left hand in 2nd inversion on the piano keyboard like this (we'll use the **C** chord to illustrate):

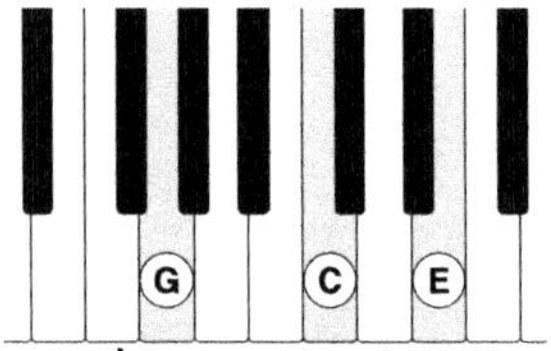

2nd inversion of C major chord

Then add the 7th to the piano chord:

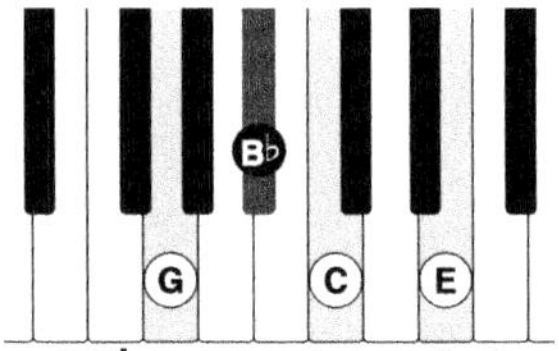

2nd inversion of C major chord

Now take your index finger off "**C**" and play "**D**" instead, like this:

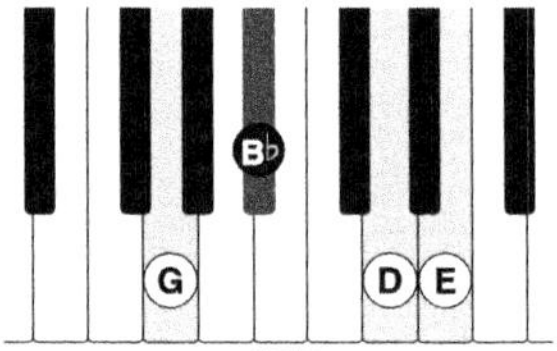

G7

You may be saying "But how could that be a **C9** chord? It doesn't have a **C** in it!"

And you would be right.

So what we need to do is to play the **C** -- the root of the chord -- an octave below middle **C** **while we depress the sustain pedal**, and *then* play the chord shown above.

Step One:

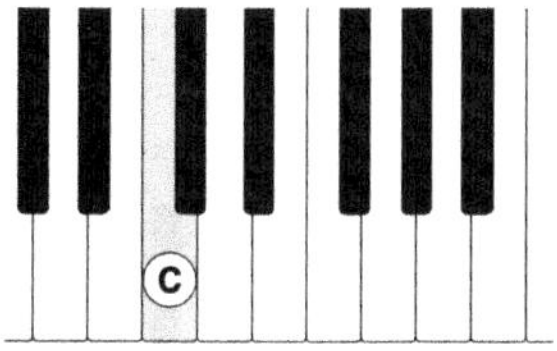

Step Two:

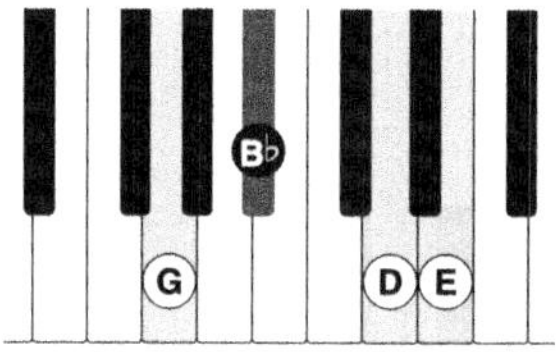

The sustain pedal **hooks the two parts together** to make one cohesive chord -- a **C9**.

So if you want to play an **F9** chord, you would play a low **F** (the root of the **F** chord) low on the keyboard, then play the **F9** chord while the sustain pedal is depressed. Same for any other 9th chord -- play the low root, *then* the chord.

Here's what *9th chords* look like on the staff:

All the 9th Chords

(Remember that accidentals carry over in the same measure!)

And here's what they look like when played with your left hand on the keyboard: (But don't forget: you **MUST** play a low note (the *root* of the chord) *before* you play the chord, then **hook them together** with your sustain pedal!)

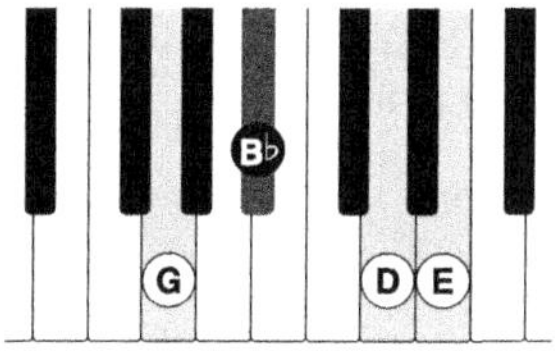

C9

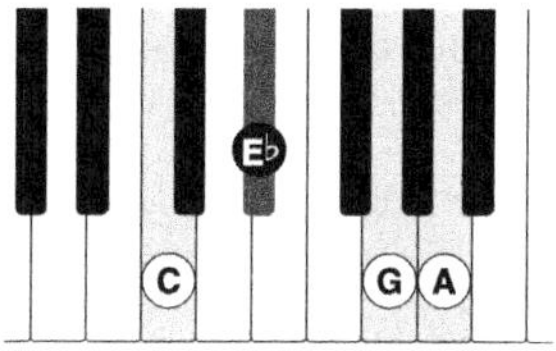

F9

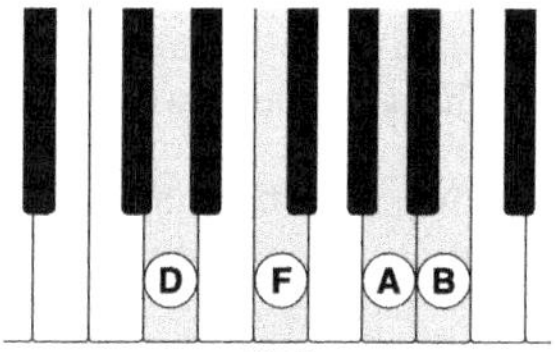

G9

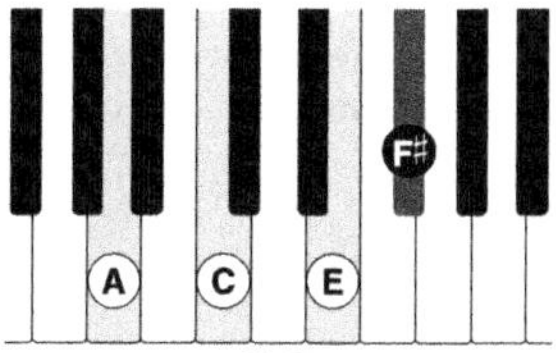

D9

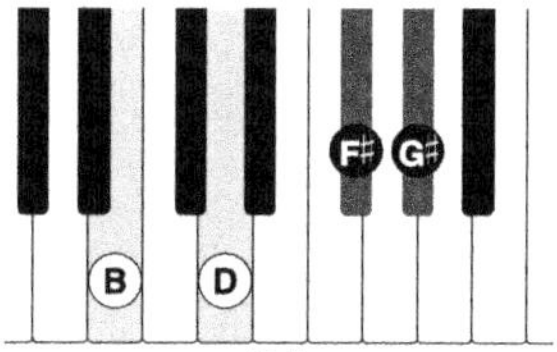

E9

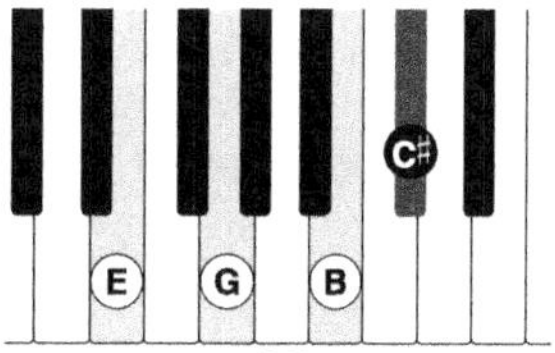

A9

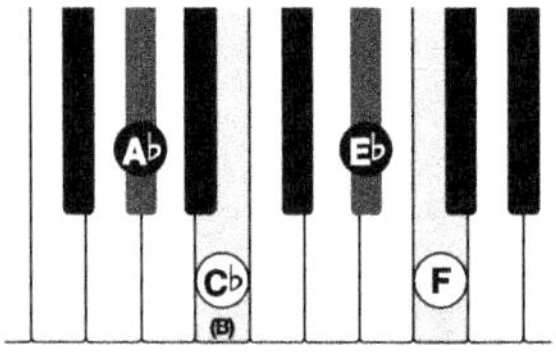

Db9

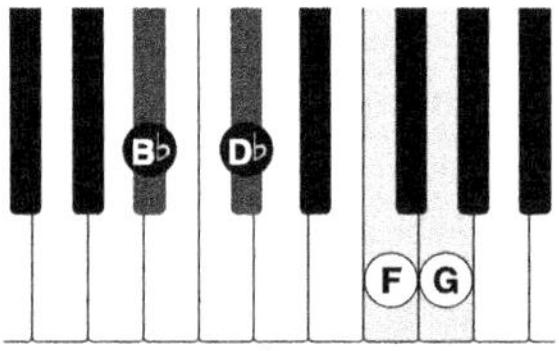

Eb9

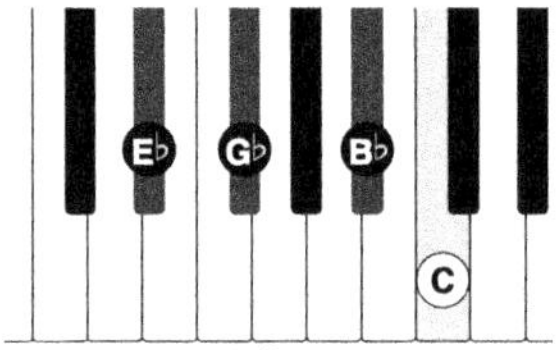

Ab9

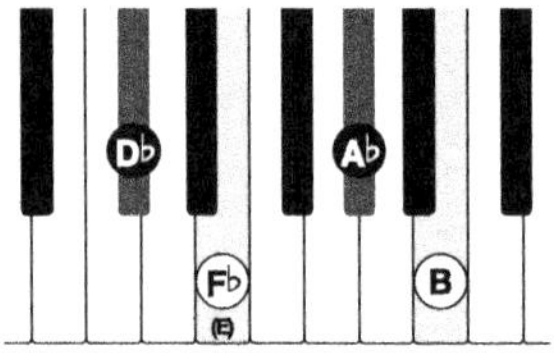

Gb9

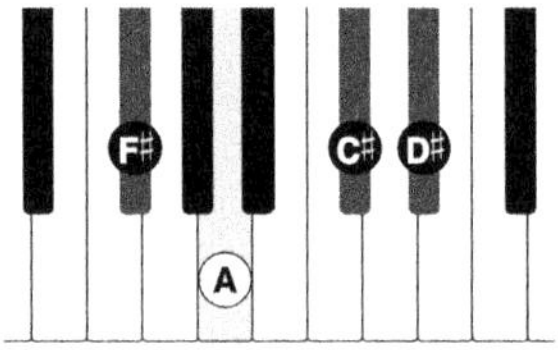

B9

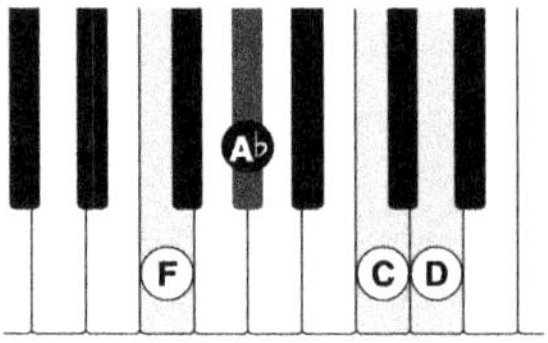

Bb9

As usual, now it's up to you. Play each 9th chord in root position, then 1st inversion, then 2nd inversion, then in 3rd inversion (the maj7th will be the lowest note of the chord). Play each chord up and down the keyboard for at least 2 octaves -- maybe 3 octaves. Play them with your left hand, then play them with your right hand. Then play them hands together.

You may be wondering if you can play 9th chords in different inversions, like you can invert 6th and 7th chords. The answer is "sure" -- but if I were you I would master one inversion before trying to use several different ones. When you're dealing with this many chords, it's easy to get turned around and confused. So unless you have a very good reason to use a different inversion, I would stick with only one inversion for now.

Go through all 12 major chords, inverting every one. Then go through all the 12 minor chords, inverting each one up and down the keyboard -- hands alone, then hands together. Then go through all 12 diminished chords, inverting each one up and down the keyboard -- each hand alone, then together. Then play the 12 augmented chords, up and down the keyboard. Then skip around from major to minor to diminished to augmented, etc.

Then add major 6th and minor 6th chords to your repertoire of chords. You know that you can turn them upside down 'till the cows come home -- invert them -- so go to it!

And then add 7th chords and their inversions....then add the maj7th chords we've learned last lesson.

Then finally, add these 9th chords into the mix -- but don't forget to play the low root before playing the chord -- **that's a must!**

Do you feel like you're getting a handle on chords yet? You ought to -- I know we're going slowly, but chords are *SO important* that you **absolutely MUST master them** if you are ever going to play the piano like you hope to!

So here's our revised chord scorecard:

12 major piano chords *to*

12 minor piano chords *to*

12 diminished piano chords *to*

12 augmented piano chords *and*

12 major 6th piano chords *and*

12 minor 6th piano chords *and*

twelve 7th piano chords *and*

twelve maj7th piano chords *and*

3 or 4 inversions of each

and now,

twelve 9th piano chords

which means you can now play **Over 365 piano chords!**

Yea! Three cheers for you!

Next lesson we will add 12 more chords to our growing list of chords we can play by adding *11th chords* to our stash.

All The 11th Piano Chords

One of the most exciting chord types you'll ever learn...

Welcome to Lesson 13. I hope you are enjoying learning about all the chords in the world -- and we're going to cover them ALL before we're done -- you'll know more about chords than 99% of the people in the world -- believe it or not, it's true.

If you recall, in Lesson 1 we learned about the three chords you absolutely, positively CAN'T do without. Then in Lesson 2 we took an airplane ride over "Chordland" just to get the lay of the land -- the overview of the world of chords. I

Lesson 3 showed you how easy it is to learn ALL the *major chords* (there are 12 of them) and be able to play them in seconds.

Next you learned how to easily turn *major chords* into *minor chords* just by moving one key one-half step -- by lowering the 3rd of the major chord.

Then we learned *diminished triads* -- just by lowering the 3rd and the 5th of a major chord 1/2 step.

Then we learned *inversions* -- how to stand chords on their head.

And finally, we took up *augmented triads* -- formed by simply raising the 5th of a major triad.

Then we learned about *major 6th chords*. They are 4-note chords -- the root, 3rd, 5th -- just like a major chord, but you also add the 6th degree of the scale to the major triad. The 6th is ALWAYS one whole step above the 5th -- never a half step -- so they are real easy to find.

Then we changed those *major 6th chords* into *minor 6th chords* just by altering the 3rd 1/2 step -- in other words, a minor triad with a 6th on top.

Then we took up *7th chords* -- very important chords, because they move you from one tonal base to another tonal base. In other words, when we move from the C chord to the F chord, we often use C7 between the two as a "connector." After that we learned about major 7th chords, and finally, 9th chords.

Today we're going to learn to form an *11th chord*. It's just like the 9th chord, except you move your left thumb up from the 3rd of the chord to the 4th -- which in this case is known as the 11th, because it includes a 9th and a 7th under it. So:

An **11th Piano Chord** = Get your chord in 2nd inversion, add the *7th* and *9th*, and also add the *11th*

Here's what 11th piano chords look like on the staff:

11th Chords

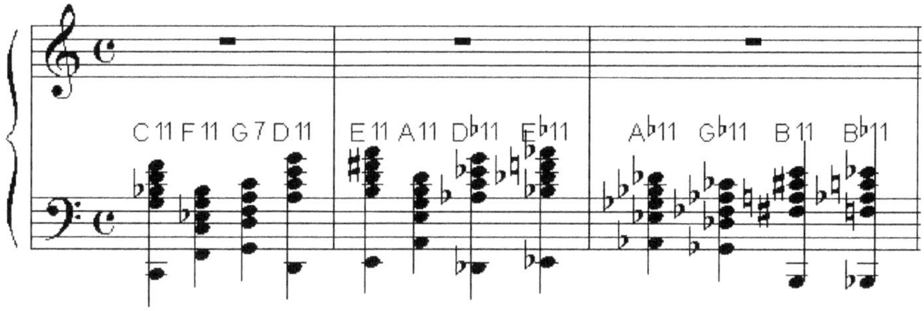

(Remember that accidentals carry over in each measure!)

The lowest note in each case is the root of the chord -- even though I have shown them above directly under the chord, be sure to play that note ***before*** *you play the chord, and use your sustain pedal to "hook the two parts together."*

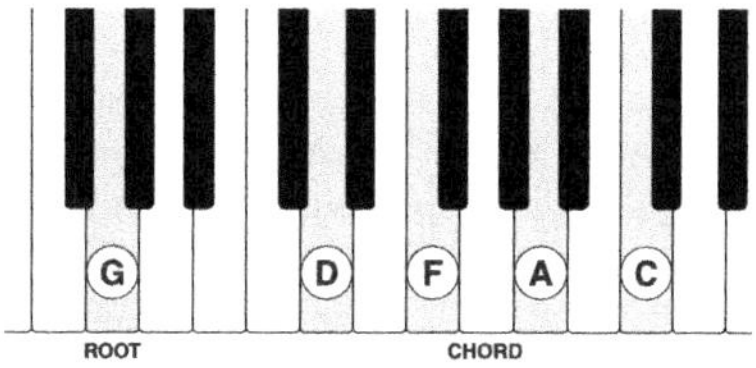

Don't forget to play a low root before playing the chord & connect them with the sustain pedal.

And here's what they look like when played with the left hand:

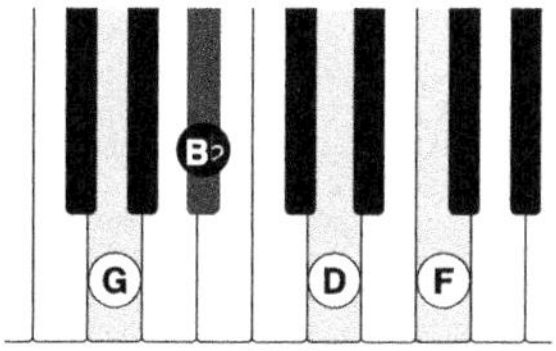

C11

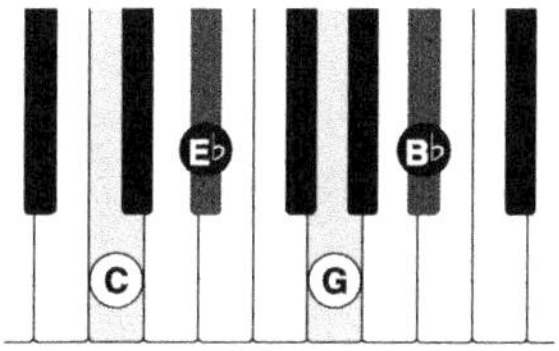

F11

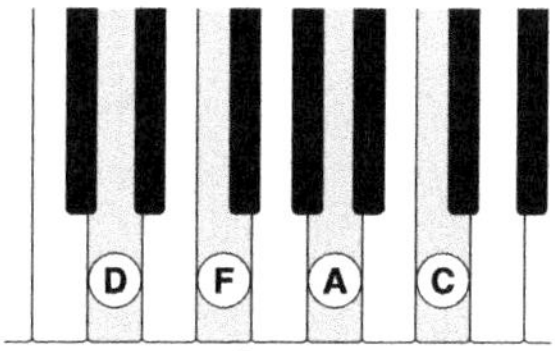

G11

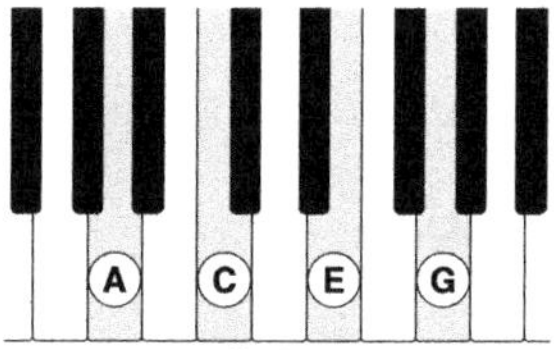

D11

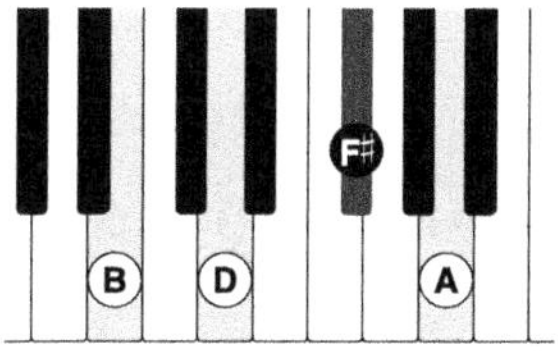

E11

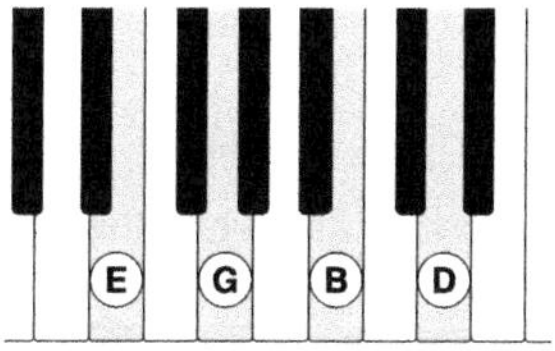

A11

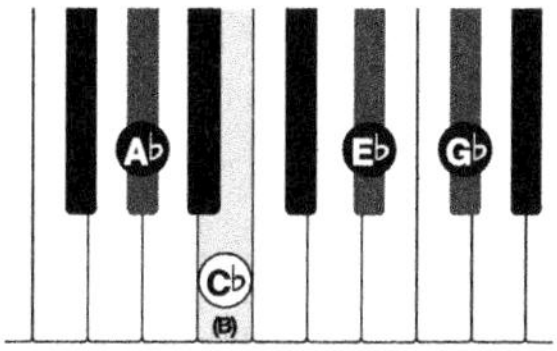

Db11

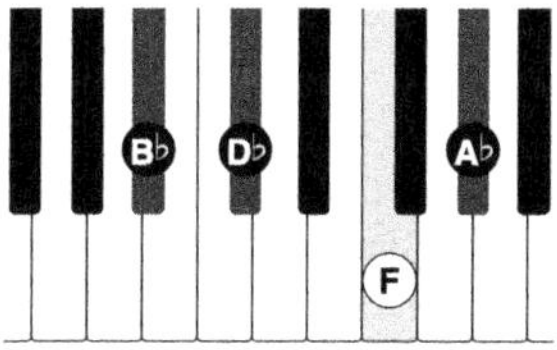

Eb11

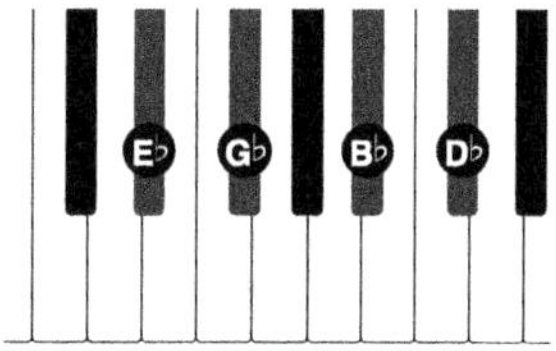

Ab11

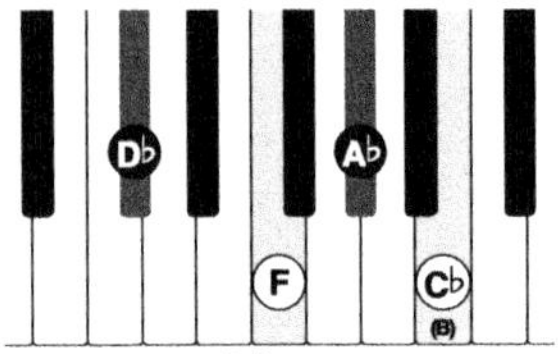

Gb11

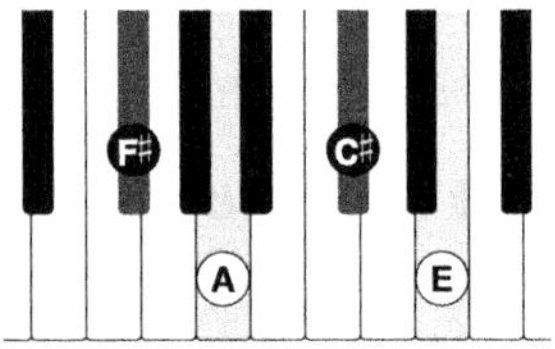

B11

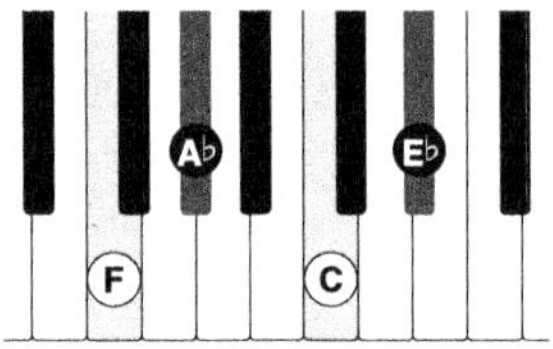

Bb11

Go through all 12 major chords, inverting every one. Then go through all the 12 minor chords, inverting each one up and down the keyboard -- hands alone, then hands together. Then go through all 12 diminished chords, inverting each one up and down the keyboard -- each hand alone, then together. Then play the 12 augmented chords, up and down the keyboard. Then skip around from major to minor to diminished to augmented, etc.

Then add major 6th and minor 6th chords to your repertoire of chords. You know that you can turn them upside down 'till the cows come home -- invert them -- so go to it!

And then add 7th chords and their inversions....then major 7th chords.....then 9th chords, and now, 11th chords.

Do you feel like you're getting a handle on chords yet? You ought to -- I know we're going slowly, but chords are *SO important* that you **absolutely MUST master them** if you are ever going to play the piano like you hope to!

So here's our revised chord scorecard:

12 major piano chords *to*

12 minor piano chords *to*

12 diminished piano chords *to*

12 augmented piano chords *and*

12 major 6th piano chords *and*

12 minor 6th piano chords *and*

a **dozen** 7th piano chords *and*

a **dozen** 9th piano chords *and now*

a **dozen** 11th piano chords *and of course you can play*

3 or 4 inversions of each

which means you can now play **at least 700 piano chords!**

In one octave, yet!

Hello! Are you doing great, or what?

Next lesson we will add 12 more chords to our growing list of piano chords we can play by adding *13th chords* to our stash. (Actually **60** more chords, since each 5-note chord such as a 13th can be inverted 5 ways -- root position, 1st inversion, 2nd inversion, 3rd inversion, and 4th inversion!)

All The 13th Piano Chords

Another one of the most exciting chord types you'll ever learn...

Welcome to Lesson 14. I hope you are enjoying learning about all the chords in the world -- and we're going to cover them ALL before we're done -- you'll know more about chords than 99% of the people in the world -- believe it or not, it's true.

If you recall, in Lesson 1 we learned about the three chords you absolutely, positively CAN'T do without. . Then in Lesson 2 we took an airplane ride over "Chordland" just to get the lay of the land -- the overview of the world of chords.

Lesson 3 showed you how easy it is to learn ALL the *major chords* (there are 12 of them) and be able to play them in seconds. In Lesson 4 you learned how to easily turn *major chords* into *minor chords* just by moving one key one-half step -- by lowering the 3rd of the major chord.

Then we learned *inversions* in Lesson 5 -- how to stand chords on their head, and we learned *diminished triads* in Lesson 6 -- just by lowering the 3rd and the 5th of a major chord 1/2 step.

With Lesson 7 we took up *augmented triads* -- formed by simply raising the 5th of a major triad, and we learned about *major 6th chords* in Lesson 8. They are 4-note chords -- the root, 3rd, 5th -- just like a major chord, but you also add the 6th degree of the scale to the major triad.

Then, in Lesson 9, we changed those *major 6th chords* into *minor 6th chords* just by altering the 3rd 1/2 step -- in other words, a minor triad with a 6th on top.

We took up *7th chords* in Lesson 10 -- very important chords, because they move you from one tonal base to another tonal base. After that we learned about *major 7th chords*, and then, *9th chords*, and then *11th chords*.

Today we're going to learn to form an 13th chord. It's just like the 11th chord, except you move your little finger up from the 5th of the chord to the 13th -- same as the 6th, except the chord includes the 7th, 9th, and 11th. So:

A **13th Piano Chord** = Get your chord in 2nd inversion, add the 7th and 9th and 11th, then bring your little finger up a whole step -- from the 5th to the 13th (same as the 6th).

Here's what 13th piano chords look like on the staff:

All the 13th Chords

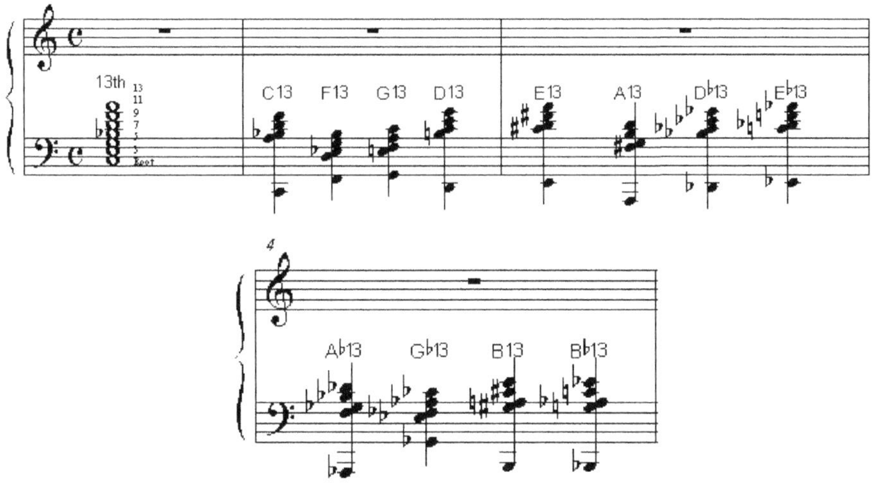

(Remember that accidentals carry over in each measure!)

The lowest note in each case is the root of the chord -- even though I have shown them above directly under the chord, be sure to play that note ***before*** *you play the chord, and use your sustain pedal to "hook the two parts together."*

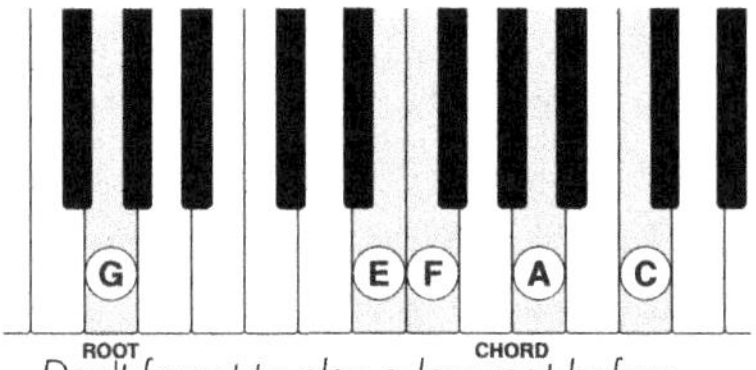

Don't forget to play a low root before playing the chord & connect them with the sustain pedal.

And here's what they look like on the staff when played with the left hand:

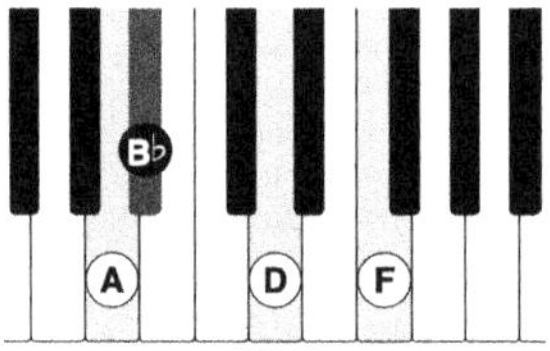

C13

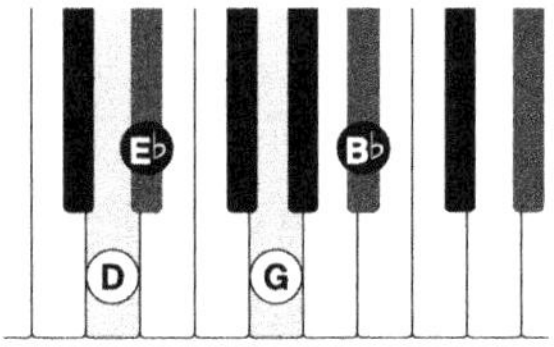

F13

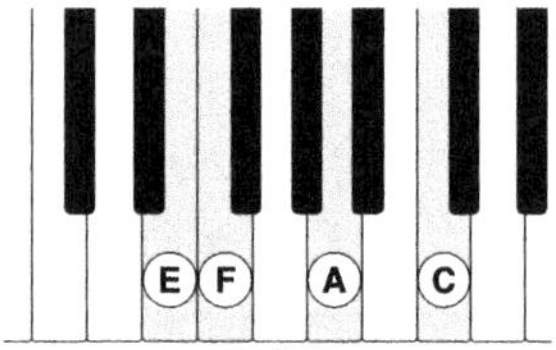

G13

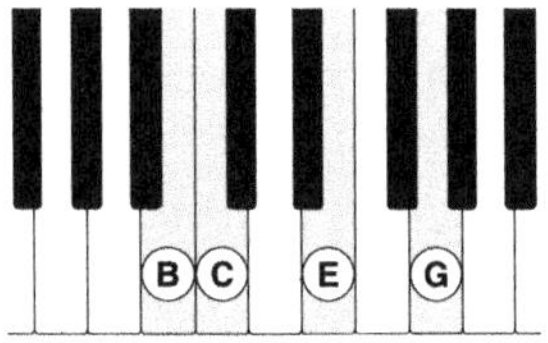

D13

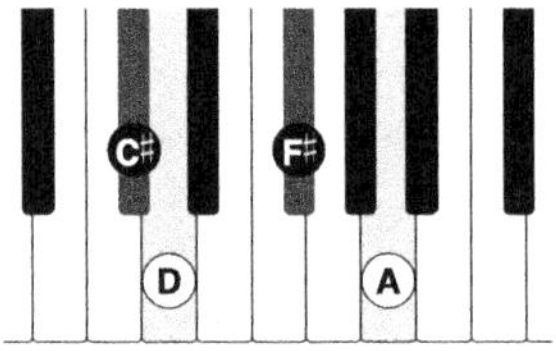

E13

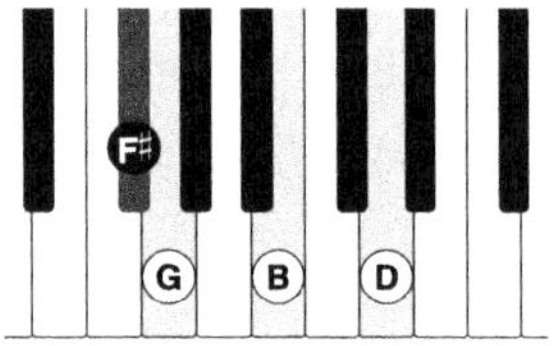

A13

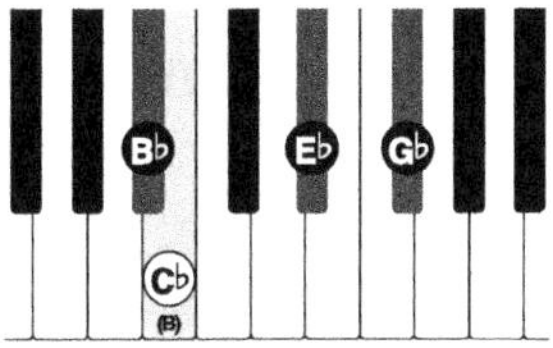

Db13

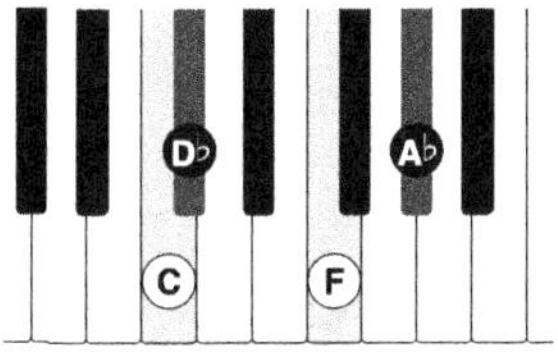

Eb13

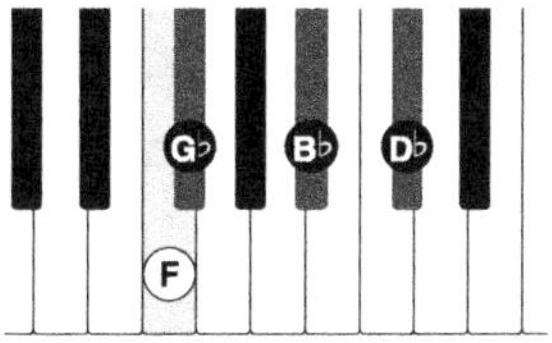

Ab13

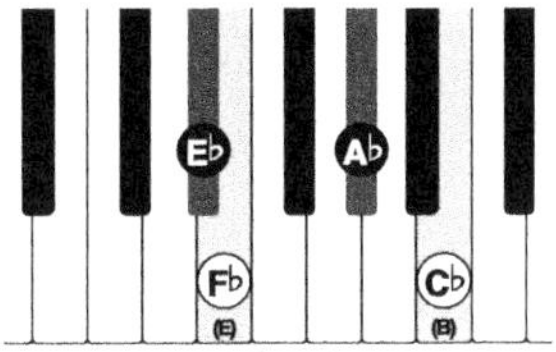

Gb13

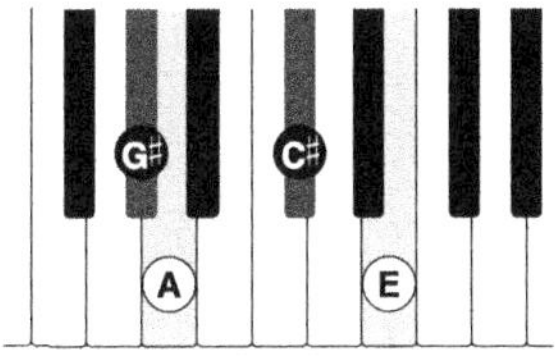

B13

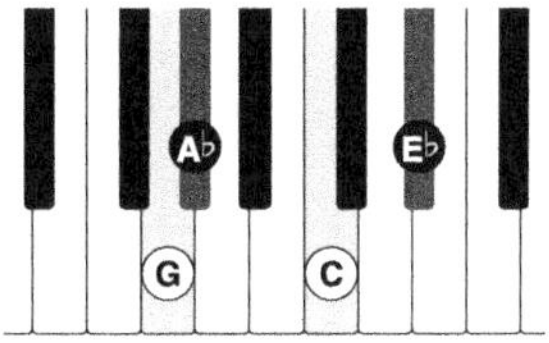

Bb13

Now - go through all 12 major chords, inverting every one. Then go through all the 12 minor chords, inverting each one up and down the keyboard -- hands alone, then hands together. Then go through all 12 diminished chords, inverting each one up and down the keyboard -- each hand alone, then together. Then play the 12 augmented chords, up and down the keyboard. Then skip around from major to minor to diminished to augmented, etc.

Then add major 6th and minor 6th chords to your rehearsal schedule.

And then add 7th chords and their inversions....then major 7th chords.....then 9th chords, 11th chords, and now, 13th chords.

Do you feel like you're getting a handle on chords yet? You ought to -- I know we're going slowly, but chords are *SO important* that you **absolutely MUST master them** if you are ever going to play the piano like you hope to!

So here's our revised chord scorecard:

12 major piano chords *to*

12 minor piano chords *to*

12 diminished piano chords *to*

12 augmented piano chords *and*

12 major 6th piano chords *and*

12 minor 6th piano chords *and*

a **dozen** 7th piano chords *and*

a **dozen** 9th chords *and*

a **dozen** 11th piano chords *and now*

one **dozen** 13th piano chords *plus*

3 or 4 inversions of each

which means you can now play **over 800 piano chords!**

In one octave, yet - and there are 7 octaves on a full piano keyboard!

Wow -- are you a genius, or what?

Next lesson we will investigate diminished 7th chords. So be sure to master 13ths before next lesson.

The 3 Diminished 7th Piano Chords

Diminished 7th chords are unique animals. They have some unusual qualities that make them interesting and useable. For example, they are the only type of chord that is simply a stack of minor 3rds. If you count from one chord note to the next, you will find that they are all equidistant.

This is what they look like on paper:

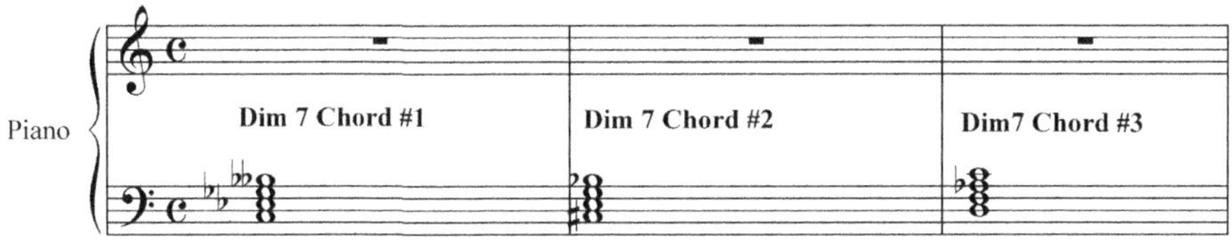

There are really *only 3* diminished 7th Piano Chords:

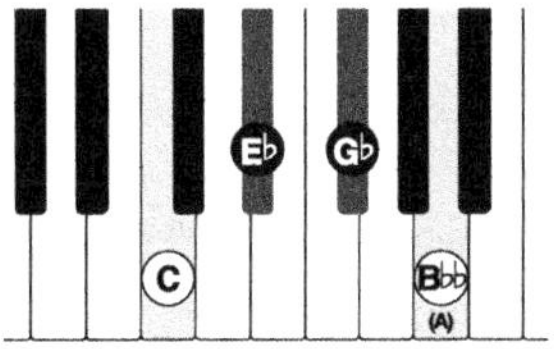

Any note in this diminished 7th chord can function as the root -- therefore this chord could be named ***Cdim7****,* ***Ebdim7****,* ***D#dim7****,* ***F#dim7****,* ***Gbdim7****,* ***Adim7****, or* ***Bbbdim7****.*

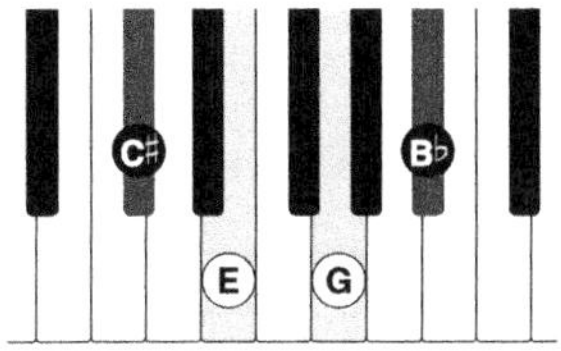

Any note in this diminished 7th chord can function as the root -- therefore this chord could be named ***C#dim7****,* ***Dbdim7****,* ***Edim7****,* ***Gdim7****,* ***A#dim7****, or* ***Bbdim7****.*

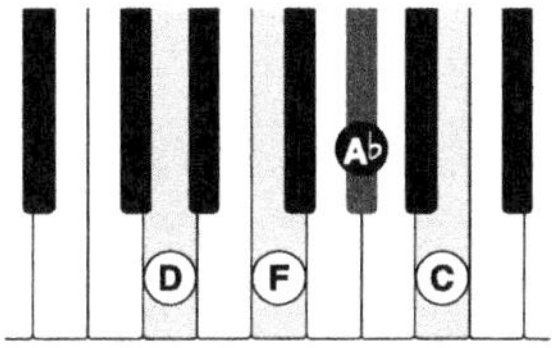

Any note in this diminished 7th chord can function as the root -- therefore this chord could be named ***Ddim7****,* ***Fdim7****,* ***G#dim7****,* ***Abdim7****,* ***Bdim7****, or* ***Cbdim7****.*

When we get into chord progressions, we will see that diminished 7th chords can be used as "*modulation agents*", "*transposition agents*", and "*transition agents*." They can transform themselves into 7th chords by just moving any one note. They can also be changed into 6th chords and major 7th chords with a minimum of movement. Each of the 3 diminished 7th chords contain two of the mysterious tri-tones, which we will take up later when we get into chord progressions. **So learn them well in ALL inversions**.

Chord Suspensions

Suspensions are chords in which the 4th degree of the scale takes the place of the 3rd degree -- usually temporarily, but not always.

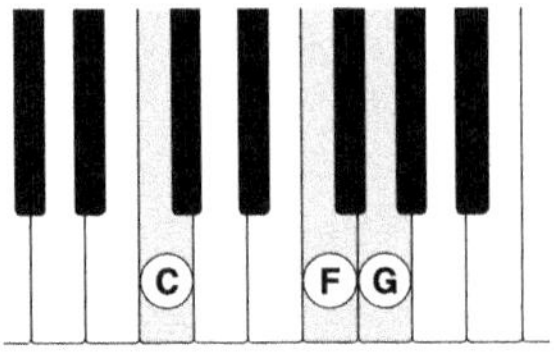

*For example, a **Csus** would look like this:*

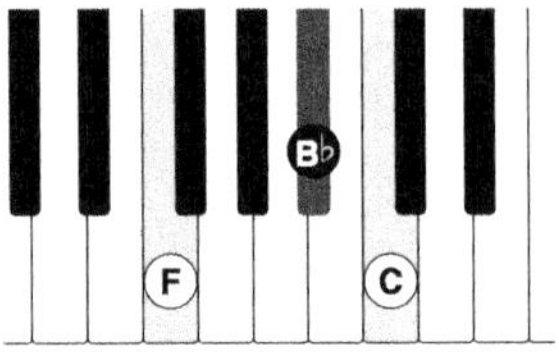

***Fsus** would look like this:*

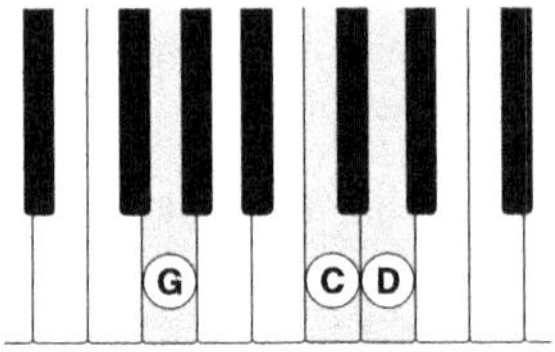

***Gsus** would look like this:*

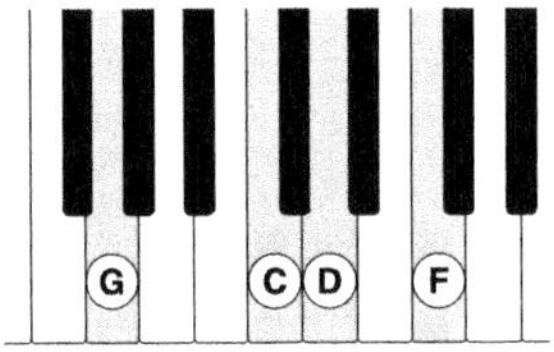

*If we had a 7th chord that was suspended, such as **G7sus**, it would look like this:*

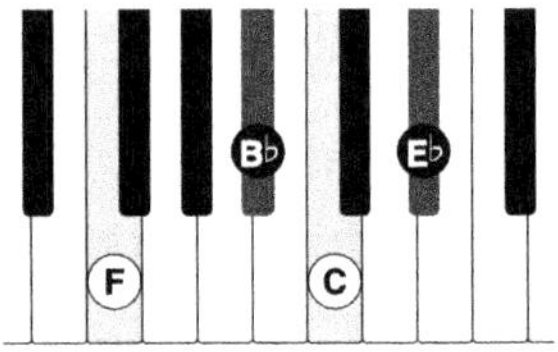

*So **F7sus** would look like this:*

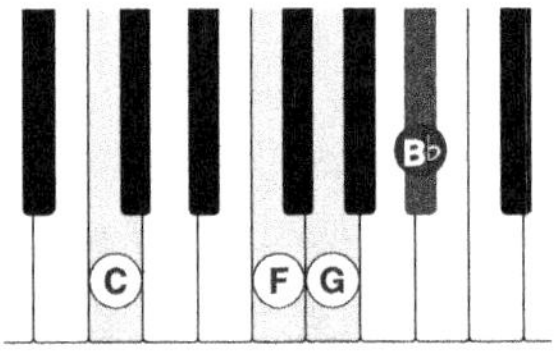

*And **C7sus** would look like this:*

It's just that easy. Replace the 3rd of the chord with the 4th, and you've got it! That's all there is to it.

Here's how these same chords look when notated:

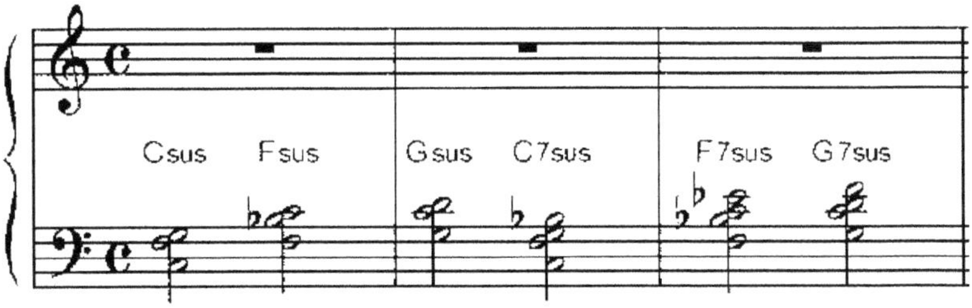

Next time we'll investigate altered chords. Meanwhile, be sure to review all the previous lessons -- from major triads to 13ths.

Alterations

So far we've covered chords from major to minor to diminished to augmented to 6ths to 7ths to maj7ths to 9ths to 11ths to 13ths -- and last time we covered suspensions. I trust that you have been MASTERING each chord type as we've gone along. We're almost through -- almost to the point where we can apply what we've learned about chords to chord progressions -- and *that's where the fun begins.*

But it won't be much fun if you can't remember the chords you've learned, so keep going over and over and over them.

Just a couple more things you need to know about chords, and one of those things is that:

Any chord can be altered through the use of a + or a -

a **+** means sharp -- *raise* the note 1/2 step

a **–** means flat -- *lower* the note 1/2 step

For example, here is a ***C7*** *chord with a flat 5th. It is notated* ***C7-5****:*

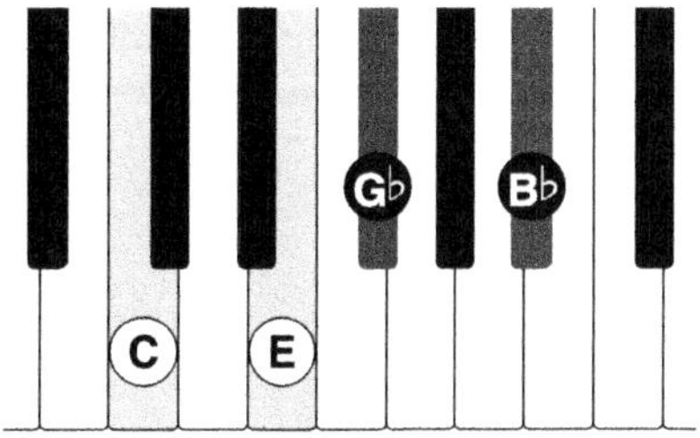

C7-5

And here is a C7 chord with a sharp 5th, notated as C7+5:

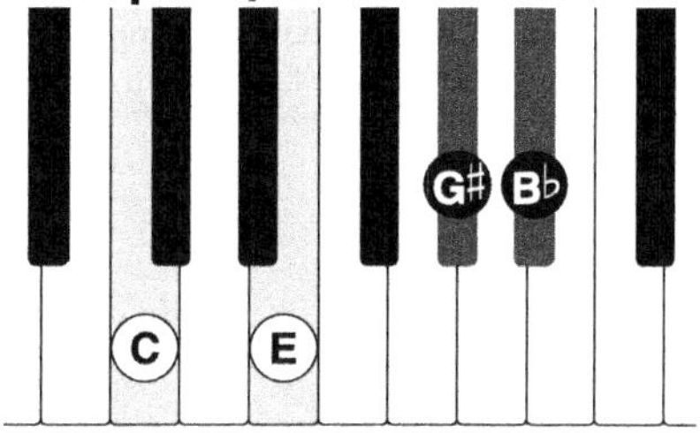

C7+5

And here is a ***C9th*** *chord in second inversion with a flat 9th, notated* ***C-9****: (But don't forget to play the low root --* ***C*** *-- first. Otherwise you have a* ***Gdim7*** *chord!)*

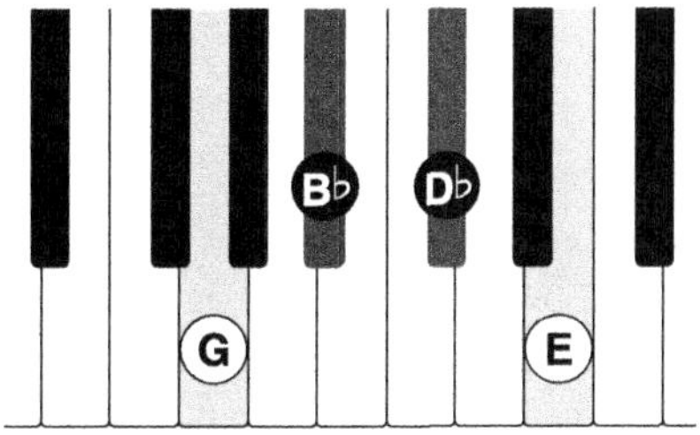

C-9
(Don't forget to play low C first)

And here we have a ***C11*** *chord, but the 11th is raised 1/2 step. So it is notated* ***C+11****:*

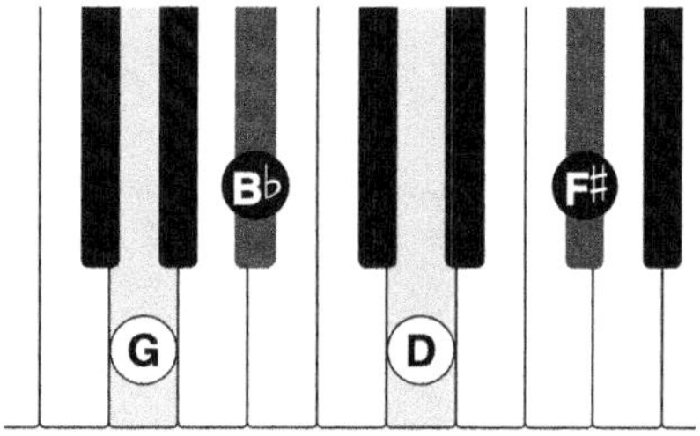

C+11
(Again – play a low root before you play this chord!)

What chord is this?

Can you figure out what this chord might be? Take a stab at it, then I'll tell you below:

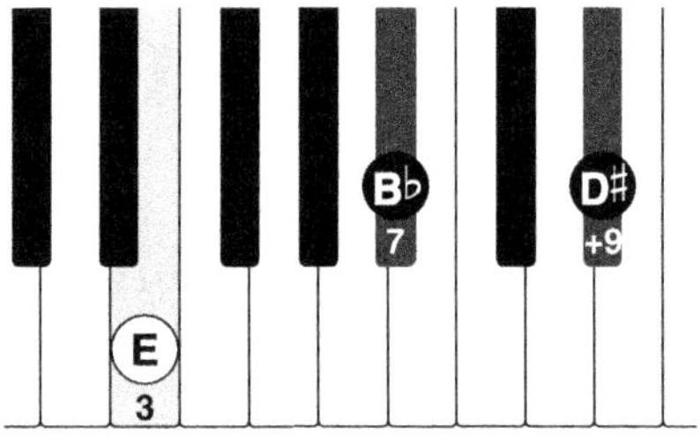

Play a low root first!

Did you figure it out? Don't feel bad if you didn't -- it's a **C+9**. You would play a low root (**C**) first and hold it with your sustain pedal, then play this chord, which is in first inversion. This is an advanced voicing -- we're leaving the 5th of the chord out, so we have a "stack of 4ths", which creates an open sound. Now that you know what it is, try it.

Sometimes -- but not often -- you'll see a symbol that says "*add 2*." That simply means to add the 2nd note of the scale (the scale of the chord you are playing) to the chord. The reason it is not called a 9th is because a 9th has a 7th under it, and this doesn't. It is notated **Cadd2** and looks like this:

That's enough for this time. I don't want you to get "musical indigestion." Next lesson we'll take a look at "slash chords" and see what they are made of, and then after that I think we're ready to being learning about the wonderful & exciting world of progressions -- the path chords take as they move from one to another.

Slash Chords

A "*slash chord*" is a hybrid kind of chord. It simply means "play the given chord OVER the note after the slash." In other words, in this example, we would have a **C** chord played, but the lowest note would be **Ab** (which of course is not in the **C** chord). What's usually going on are "passing tones" that comprise a type of counter melody.

Here's an example of a "slash chord":

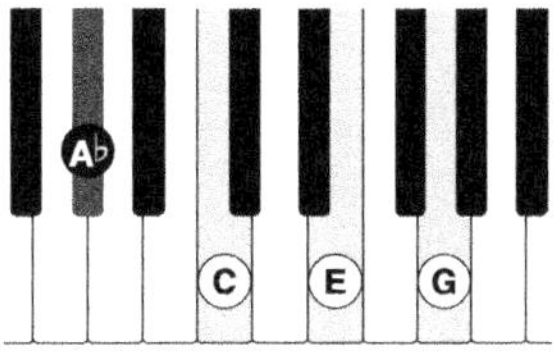

Slash chords are just chords that have a bottom note other than the root -- sometimes notes that aren't in the chord at all. So you might encounter:

Cm7/Bb - F6/C - G9/F - Eb13/Ab - A7/G - etc.

Try all those on for size. Just remember that the letter to the **left** tells *what chord it is*, and the letter **after the "slash"** tells what *the lowest note of the chord* should be.

Chord name/Lowest note

And that's all you need to know about that!

Oops! I forgot Minor 7th Chords!

How could I do it? *Minor 7th chords* are some of the **most-used chords** there are. They are also the mellowest chords around -- entire songs have been composed using nothing but minor 7th chords, and even more songs composed with a combination of minor 7ths and maj7th chords.

So don't think they are not important. Just chalk it up to the fact that it's easy to overlook the obvious. And that's exactly what I did.

Minor 7th chords are made of a *minor 3rd* with a *major third* over it and a *minor 3rd* over that. In other words, every other interval is minor, and every other interval is major.

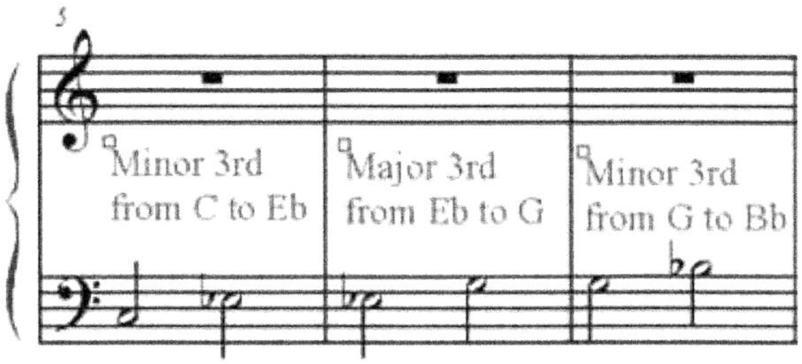

For example, on **Cm7** it is a minor 3rd from **C** to **Eb**. Then it is a major 3rd from **Eb** to **G**. Then it is a minor 3rd from **G** to **Bb**.

And here's what they look like:

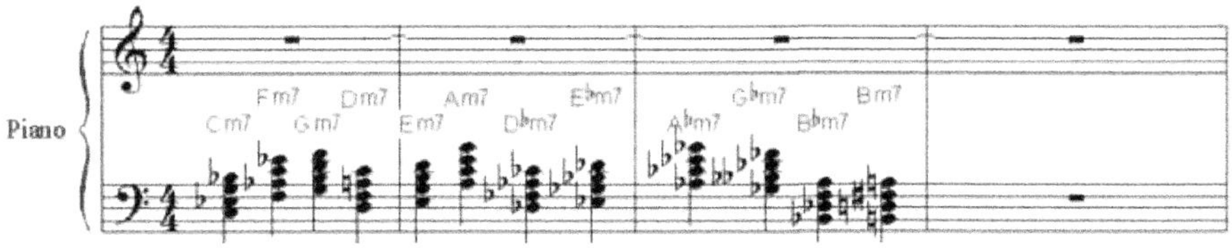

Play them over and over until you get the feel of each one. Then try playing them with your left hand while playing one or more of them broken in the right hand. **That's the very beginning of improvisation!**

Chord Progressions Part One

The Circle of Keys - Major

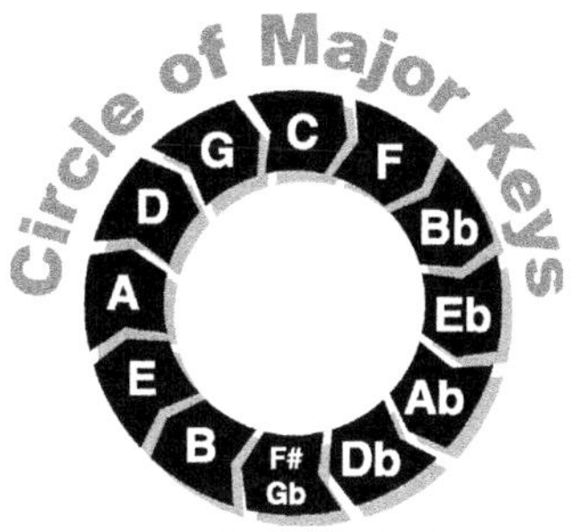

Circle of 4ths
Circle of 5ths

If you've ever heard of the "*circle of 4ths*" or the "*circle of 5ths*", they are the same thing as the "*circle of keys.*" It just depends on whether you're moving clockwise or counter-clockwise around the circle.

All the major keys that you can play in -- 12 of 'em -- are listed in this circle. Take a look for yourself:

Major Keys:

C F Bb Eb Ab Db Gb B E A D G

So "**C**" is at the top of your circle, and **Gb** (same as **F#**) is at the bottom of your circle.

Now memorize that circle. You'll soon notice that each letter is a *4th above* the previous letter -- hence, the "*circle of 4ths.*" Or if you go the other way, you'll soon notice that each letter is a *5th above* the previous letter -- hence, the "*circle of 5ths.*"

This is the way chords "want" to move -- up a 4th. Or up a 5th. You will find those to be the most common chord progression of all -- up a 4th from the previous chord, or up a 5th from the previous chord.

For example, if the chord you are playing is **C**, the most likely chord to occur next is either **F** or **G**. You will notice that **F** comes directly to the right of **C** on the circle, and **G** directly to the left. (And you do remember, don't you, that **C**, **F**, and **G** are the "*family chords*" of the **Key of C**? -- the primary chords -- therefore, the most likely chords to occur? -- Now you know why!)

So that means that at any point on the circle you can immediately know the most likely chords -- the chord to the left, and the chord to the right! Here's a quiz:

What are the 3 most likely chords in the key of **Db**?

Right.

Db (of course), plus the chords on either side of it -- **Ab** and **Gb**.

So what we come out with is this -- the most likely chords in each key:

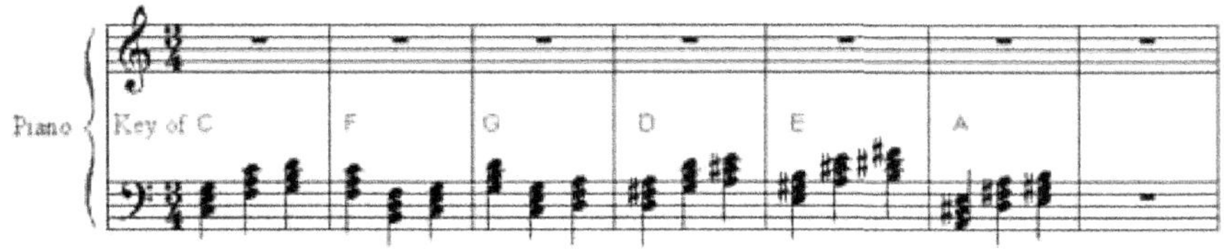

Do you see what an enormous advantage this gives you? You have a *highly educated guess* what chords are going to occur in the song you are playing based on the key that the song is written in. Not only that, you now know that chords like to either move up a 4th or a 5th (or down a 4th or 5th -- same thing).

And so as we begin learning chord progressions, this is the first step -- memorize the circle above until you can say it forward and backward and upside down and in your sleep! If I were you, I would print it out and stick it up on your piano or bathroom mirror or wherever you would see it often -- ***it's that important***.

That's all for this time.

Next lesson we'll take a look at the Circle of Minor Keys -- giving you the same insight in any minor key.

Chord Progressions Part Two

The Circle of Minor Keys

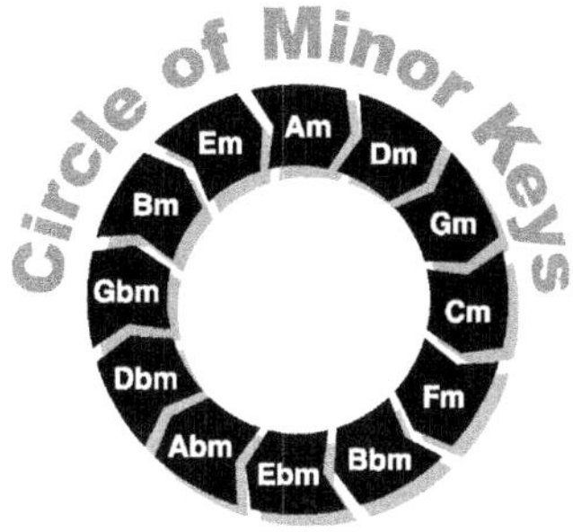

Last week we looked at the "*circle of 4ths*" or the "*circle of 5ths*", they are the same thing as the "*circle of keys.*" It just depends on whether you're moving clock-wise or counter-clockwise around the circle. All the major keys that you can play in -- 12 of 'em -- are listed in this circle:

Major Keys:

C F Bb Eb Ab Db Gb B E A D G

But there are also *12 minor keys* in which songs can be written, so there must also be a "*circle of minor keys.*" It's not as well known as the "circle of major keys", but it works the same way. Here it is:

It works the same way as the major circle of keys, *with one exception*:

When figuring the 3 most likely chords in any key, you still look left and look right, but because of the fact that most songs written in the western hemisphere use the harmonic minor scale instead of the natural minor scale (which is much too involved to get into here -- if you want to know about that in detail you'll need to get a course on scales), the chord to the left is usually a MAJOR chord instead of a minor chord.

So in the key of **Am**, the 3 most likely chords would be **Am**, **Dm**, and ***E major*** -- not ***E minor***! There are some exceptions to that, but not many.

So what we come out with is this -- the most likely chords in each minor key:

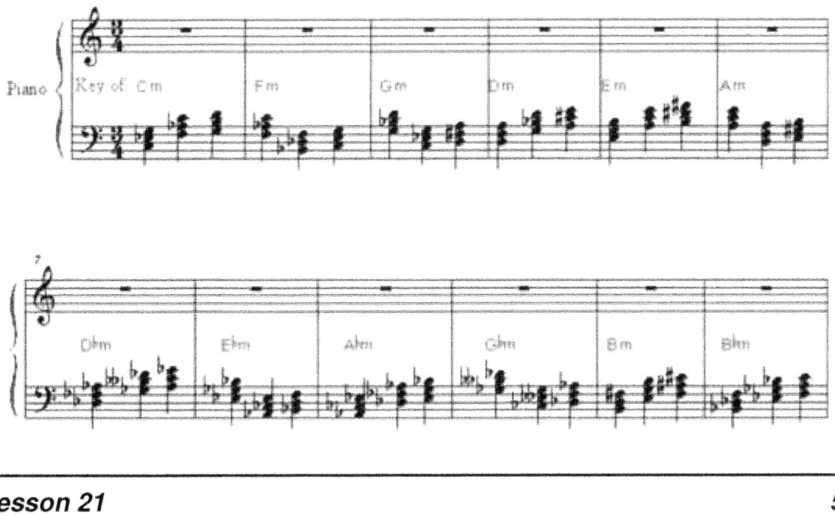

So -- to repeat from the last lesson:

Do you see what an enormous advantage this gives you? You have a *highly educated guess* what chords are going to occur in the song you are playing based on the key that the song is written in. Not only that, you now know that chords like to either move up a 4th or a 5th (or down a 4th or 5th -- same thing).

And so as we begin learning chord progressions, this is the first step -- memorize the circle above until you can say it forward and backward and upside down and in your sleep! If I were you, I would print it out and stick it up on your piano or bathroom mirror or wherever you would see it often -- ***it's that important***.

That's all for this time.

Next lesson we'll see how you can quickly tell what key a song is in, therefore telling you in advance what chords are the most likely! Is that important?

It is huge -- monumental -- galactic! Don't miss it!

Chord Progressions Part Three

How To Tell What Key You Are In When You Have Flats (b) In The Key Signature!

If you're going to be able to know what chord progressions are likely in each key, you obviously need to know how to find the key of a song quickly -- *correct*?

Here's how to instantly find what key you are in when there are flats in the key signature of a song:

Did you know that the flats in any key signature always occur in the same order? Once you know that order, you will never again wonder "Which notes are flat in this song?"

They always occur in this order in any key signature:

B E A D G C F

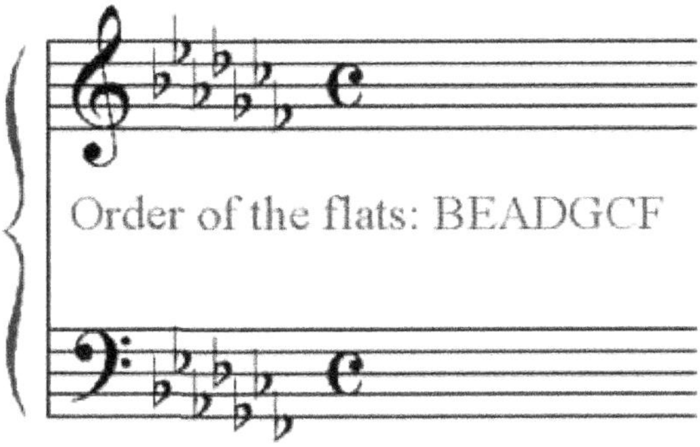
Order of the flats: BEADGCF

Notice that the first four flats spell the word "**BEAD**." You can remember the last 3 flats by making up some silly saying such as "**G**o **C**atch **F**ish" or any similar phrase that grabs your fancy.

So if there is one flat in the key signature, what is it?

Right. **Bb**.

If there are two flats in the key signature, they are what?

Right again. **Bb** and **Eb**.

How about 5 flats?

Sure. **BEAD** and **G**.

You got it. That's all there is to it.

To find what key you're in, just take the next to the last flat and that IS the key. For example, if you have 4 flats, they would be **Bb Eb Ab Db**. The next to the last flat is **Ab**, so you're in the key of **Ab**.

If you have 2 flats, they are **Bb** and **Eb**, so the next to the last flat is **Bb**-- therefore the key is **Bb**.

If you have 3 flats, they are **Bb**, **Eb** and **Ab**. Since **Eb** is the second to the last flat, the key is **Eb**.

If there is only 1 flat in the key signature, it would of course be **Bb**, and you'll just have to memorize that it is the key of **F**.

And you no doubt already know that if you have no flats or sharps in the key signature, you are in the key of C major (or A minor -- but we'll take that option up later).

Get this down cold -- so you immediately know what key you're in when you have flats in the key signature of a song. Why? Because once you know what key you are in, you also know which 3 chords are the most likely -- right?

Next week we'll do the same thing with sharp keys, so you can know immediately what the key is and therefore what the 3 most likely chords are!

Chord Progressions Part Four

How To Tell What Key You Are In When You Have Sharps (#) In The Key Signature!

If you're going to be able to know what chord progressions are likely in each key, you obviously need to know how to find the key of a song quickly -- *correct*?

Here's how to **instantly** find what key you are in when there are sharps in the key signature of a song:

You know that the flats in any key signature always occur in the same order - **BEADGCF**.

Sharps also occur in the same order -- except that order is BACKWARDS from the order of the flats. Instead of **BEADGCF**, the order of the sharps is:

F C G D A E B

They always occur in that order in a key signature. You can memorize them by saying the flats backward, or make up a silly saying of some kind such as Fat Cats Go Down Alleys Eating Bologna.

All you do to find the key is:

Go up 1/2 step from the last sharp
= that IS the key

And you already know that if you have no flats or sharps in the key signature, you are in the key of **C major** (or **A minor** -- but we'll take that option up later).

Get this down cold -- so you immediately know what key you're in when you have sharps in the key signature of a song. Why? Because once you know what key you are in, you also know which 3 chords are the most likely -- right?

Now that you know how to find the key of a song, it's time to get into chord progressions proper. Tune in same time, same station, next lesson, when we'll take up our first chord progression named "**Oh Duh!**"

Chord Progressions Part Five

The 'Oh Duh!' Chord Progression

I think we have laid the foundation for understanding chord progressions now. We have covered chords from basic triads to extended, altered, suspended, and slash chords. We have learned how the circle of keys works in both major and minor keys. And we have learned how to tell what key a song is in when there are flats in the key signature, when there are sharps in the key signature, and when there is neither.

So let's begin learning some of the most used chord progressions -- the progressions that happen over and over and over again in song after song after song.

The first progression we will consider I have labeled the "Oh Duh!" chord progression. When my daughter, Kendra, was in junior high school, she and her friends used to use that term a lot. Whenever I said something overly obvious, she would say "Oh Duh!" -- meaning, of course, that whatever I said was so painfully obvious that it really didn't need to be said at all. And that's exactly what this chord progression is -- so obvious that it hardly needs to be mentioned.

Except it DOES need to be mentioned, because most people don't know the fundamentals that YOU now know -- they don't know that there are 3 chords in any key that are MUCH more likely to be used than any others. We call them primary chords -- the I, IV, and V chords.

Just to briefly review, here they are again -- the 3 most used chords -- the primary chords -- in each major key:

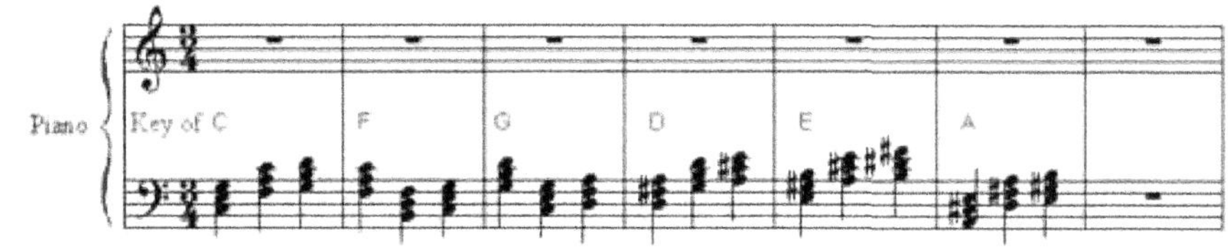

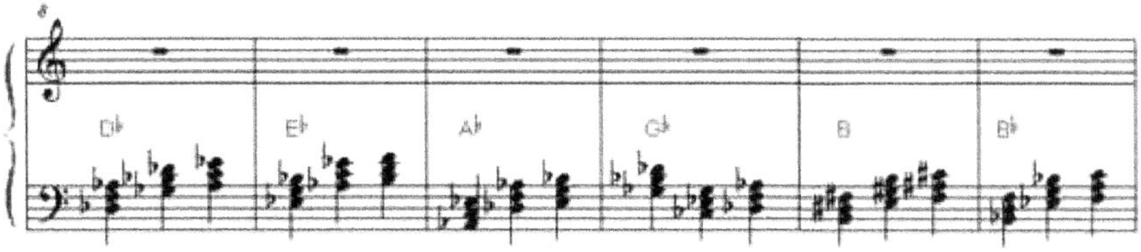

So if a song you want to play is in the key of **C**, what are the chords you would expect to find most?

Right -- **C**, **F**, and **G**.

We also know that the **I** chord is THE most used chord in that key, and songs nearly always (probably 90% of the time) start and end on the **I** chord.

So if you determine that a song is in the key of **F**, what is far and away the most likely chord?

Of course. **F**.

What chord would you expect the song to start on?

Of course. **F**.

What chord would you expect the song to end on?

Again, **F**.

So after the first chord, there are just two possibilities for the 2nd chord. Either the **IV** chord or the **V** chord. (It might be any chord if you care to get picky, but we're speaking here in mathematical terms. The likelihood of the second chord of a song being anything other than **IV** or **V** is small, so if you were betting, you would certainly bet on **IV** or **V**.)

So the obvious question then is:

> "*How can I tell whether the second chord is the* **IV** *chord or the* **V** *chord?*"

And the answer is:

> "*What's the melody note at that point? Is it part of the* **IV** *chord, or part of the* **V** *chord?*"

If the melody note is a member of the **IV** chord, then....

Oh Duh! The chord is the **IV** chord!

If on the other hand the melody note is a member of the **V** chord, then...

Oh Duh! The chord is the **V** chord!

Here's a tune in the Key of **C**. The first few notes (**C**, **E**, **G**) are all members of the **C** chord -- correct? Since we expect any song in the Key of **C** to start with the **I** chord, we have "double evidence" that the first chord is indeed **C** because the tune spells out the **C** chord.

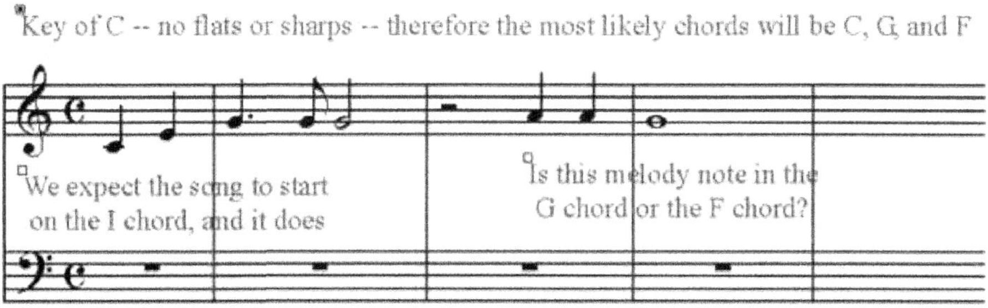

Key of C -- no flats or sharps -- therefore the most likely chords will be C, G, and F
We expect the song to start on the I chord, and it does
Is this melody note in the G chord or the F chord?

Oh Duh!

When the melody uses a note that *is NOT* part of the **I** chord, then we have to guess whether the next chord will be a **IV** chord or a **V** chord -- correct?

What is the melody note?

It's an "**A**." Is that part of the **V** chord or the **IV** chord?

Right! It's part of the **IV** chord -- **F** -- which consists of three notes: **F**, **A**, **C**.

It's NOT part of the **V** chord -- **G** -- which consists of three notes: **G**, **B**, **D**.

All together now:

Oh Duh!

You may be wondering "But what if the melody is **C** -- that's part of the **I** chord as well as part of the **IV** chord!" That's right. That's where your ear comes in. If you feel a change of chords, then change it. If you don't feel a change of chords, don't change it. **Duh!** If you can't hear the difference, then it doesn't matter.

So you use your brain -- what you know about chords -- along with your ear.

Together they are a dynamite combination.

Chord Progressions Part Six

What You Need To Know About Musical Form

Chord progressions come in sections, like one room in a house. You can put several different rooms together to make a big house, or you can live in a one room house. Just like people. In most 3rd world countries people live in one room houses -- which means, of course, that much of the world lives in one-room houses. Those of us who live in the West generally live in multi-room houses.

But there are also musical houses -- we call them songs -- that are built out of several different rooms -- several different chord progressions. Some of them, like mansions and castles, go on and on and get quite involved.

But most songs are like many modest houses -- they have 2 or 3 rooms, sometimes 4 -- built using 2 or 3 or 4 different chord progressions.

Each "room" in a musical house is called a theme, or a "motif." The first theme is always called "**A**." The next theme is called "**B**", the next theme is called "**C**", and so on. Most songs only have 2 or 3 themes, but these themes often repeat.

For example, let's say we have a chord progression that goes like this:

C Am7 Dm7 G7

...and then it repeats those same 4 chords...

and then we have another chord progression that goes like this:

Gm7 C7 F Fm7 Bb7 Eb G7

...and then the first chord progression is used again as the song ends.

This song would have a musical form of **A**, **A**, **B**, **A** -- main theme, repeat of main theme, contrasting theme, main theme.

Theme - Theme - *Contrast* - Theme

This form is known as **A A B A** musical form.

If the song went like this:

Theme - *Contrast* - Theme

...it would be known at **A B A** musical form.

The "**B**" section of a song is sometimes called the "*bridge*", or the "*release*", or the "*chorus*." These terms usually mean the same thing -- depending upon the form used.

Can you guess what *this* might be called?

Theme - *Contrast* - Theme - *Contrast* - Theme - *Contrast* - Theme - *Contrast*

Right you are! **A B A B** form. This is also known as "*verse-chorus*" form.

Most popular songs fall into one of these forms:

A B A

A A B A

A B A C A

A B A B

Why should you care?

Because if you know songs are constructed this way, you can look at songs with *smart eyes* -- you know what to look for, and once you determine the form, you have a "*mental map*" of the song -- you're not just wandering from chord to chord anymore.

In addition, most songs are proportional. That is -- 4 bars of section **A**, then 4 bars of section **B**, then another 4 bars of section **A**, and so on. You will find TONS and TONS of popular songs that are 32 bars long in **A A B A** form -- 8 bars of theme **A**, 8 bars of theme **A** repeated, then a bridge of 8 bars, finishing with 8 bars of theme **A**.

Does that give you an advantage knowing that?

It gives you a HUGE advantage because you know what to look for, and you know that if you learn theme A you have automatically learned 75% of the song! All that remains is to learn the 8 bars of the bridge, and you've got it!

And that's why you need to learn about form.

Chord Progressions Part Seven

The 'Creep' Chord Progression

Last lesson we learned the most obvious chord progression of all:

The "**Oh Duh**" Chord Progression

1. If there are 3 primary chords in a key -- **I**, **IV**, and **V** -- *and there are*;
2. And since most songs start and end on the **I** chord -- *and they do*;
3. Then the obvious conclusion is that there are *only two* possibilities for the next chord -- the **V** chord or the **IV** chord;
4. So if the melody note *is part of the* **V** *chord*, then the chord is *probably the* **V** *chord.* (**Duh!**) If the melody is not part of the V chord, then the chord is probably the IV chord. (**Duh!**)

Just to briefly review, here they are again -- the 3 most used chords -- the primary chords -- in each major key:

This time we're going to learn the "*creep*" chord progression, using those diminished 7th chords we learned back a few lessons ago. I call it the "creep" because the chords creep up gradually until you arrive at a stable chord, then the song goes elsewhere.

You see, chord progressions come in sections, like one room in a house. You can put several different rooms together to make a big house, or you can live in a one room house. Just like people. In most 3rd world countries people live in one room houses -- which means, of course, that much of the world lives in one-room houses (we won't count bathrooms and closets, etc. -- just the main living area.) Those of us who live in the West generally live in multi-room houses.

Chord progressions are like that. You can build an entire song out of one progression, such as the "**Oh Duh**" progression that we learned last time. And thousands of songs are built that way. Here's just a few:

Amazing Grace	***Dixie***
On Top Of Old Smoky	***Battle Hymn Of The Republic***
Cum Ba Ya	***Home Sweet Home***
Yankee Doodle	***Long Long Ago***
America	***Clementine***

And about *17 gazillion more...*

But there are also musical houses -- we call them songs -- that are built out of several different rooms -- several different chord progressions. Some of them, like mansions and castles, go on and on and get quite involved.

But most songs are like many modest houses -- they have 2 or 3 rooms, sometimes 4 -- built using 2 or 3 or 4 different chord progressions.

Here's an example of the "*creep*" chord progression:

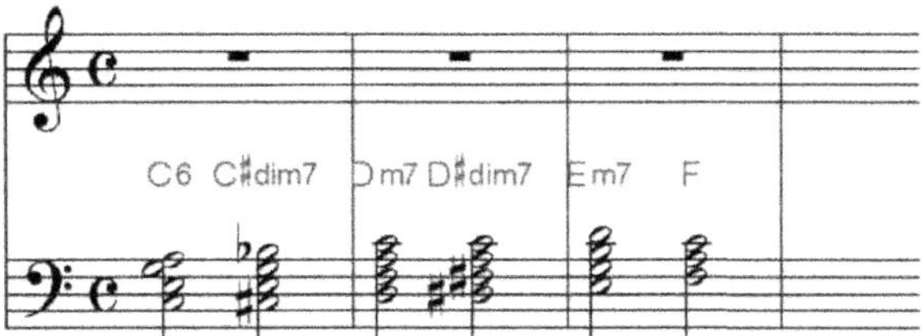
C6 C#dim7 Dm7 D#dim7 Em7 F

Creeping up by 1/2 steps until a stable chord is reached - F - a primary chord.

Once the progression reaches a stable chord -- usually a primary chord -- then it can be combined with one or more other progressions to create an entire song.

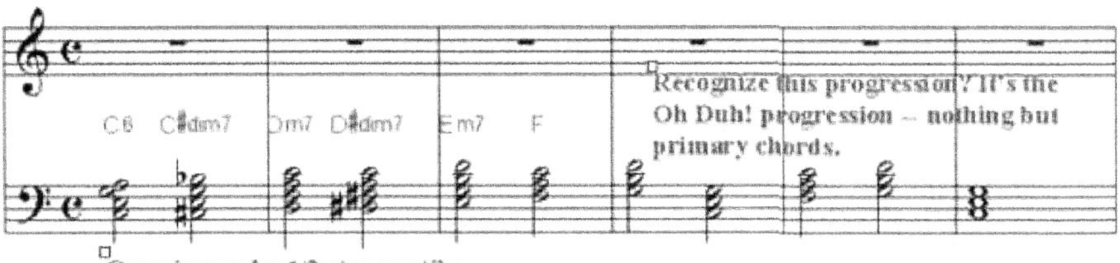
C6 C#dim7 Dm7 D#dim7 Em7 F
Recognize this progression? It's the Oh Duh! progression -- nothing but primary chords.

Creeping up by 1/2 steps until a stable chord is reached - F - a primary chord.

So here we have the "*creep*" combined with the "**Oh Duh!**" chord progression to form an entire phrase. If it is the first phrase of the song, it would be called the "theme" of the song, or "Section A" of a song. Typically in a song, a phrase like this is repeated several times in one of these musical forms:

Theme - Theme - *Contrast* - Theme

This form is known as **A A B A** musical form.

If the song went like this:

Theme - *Contrast* - Theme

...it would be known as **A B A** musical form.

Every song has a form of some kind, so you can do yourself a HUGE favor and begin to look at songs with an eye to figuring out their musical form!

Why?

Because if you can recognize a song as an **A A B A** form song, all you have to do is determine the chord progression of the "**A**" section, and you've *automatically* learned 3/4 of the song! All that remains is learning the "**B**" section, and ***you've got it!***

Chord Progressions Part Eight

The 'II - V7 - I' Chord Progression

In an earlier lesson we established the foundation for chord prediction by learning the primary chords for each key. I hope you internalized that and committed each "*family of chords*" to memory.

Now that you know "*the fam*", I would like to introduce you to the "*cousin*" chords. These are chords that don't occur near as often as the primary chords, but much more often than "*neighbor*" chords, and way more often than "*stranger*" chords.

The most likely cousin-chord to show up in any key is the **II** chord. In other words, after the **I**, **IV**, and **V** chords, the **II** chord is the next most likely to be used. It might show up in one of several forms -- it might be a *major* chord, it might be a *minor* chord, it might be a *7th chord* -- but however it shows up, it is far and away the most likely chord to occur after **I**, **IV**, or **V**.

So in the key of **C**, that means that some form of the **D** chord is the 4th most likely chord to occur. Maybe **D7**, maybe **Dm7**, maybe just **D**, but *whatever the form*, it is like the cousin that likes to show up at dinner time to eat with the fam. And when it does occur, you can then predict with uncanny accuracy which chord will come after it -- *the* **V** *chord*. And after that, the **I** chord.

*So if you were a betting person, your odds would go sky high at that point for that succession of chords to occur. In musical terms, this progression is known as the **II** - **V** -- **I** chord progression. And it happens over and over and over and over again in countless songs.*

So let's **get it down cold**. If it happens so much, it's worth your time to master it both intellectually and hand-wise (in other words, understand it and be able to play it).

Here's the **II**, **V**, **I** progression in all keys:

Key of **C**: **D G C**

Key of **F**: **G C F**

Key of **G**: **A D G**

Key of **D**: **E A D**

Key of **E**: **F# B E**

Key of **A**: **B E A**

Key of **Gb**: **Ab Db Gb**

Key of **Db**: **Eb Ab Db**

Key of **Eb**: **F Bb Eb**

Key of **Ab**: **Bb Eb Ab**

Key of **B**: **C# F# B**

Key of **Bb**: **C F Bb**

And here's what the progression looks like in the keys of **C**, **F**, and **Bb**:

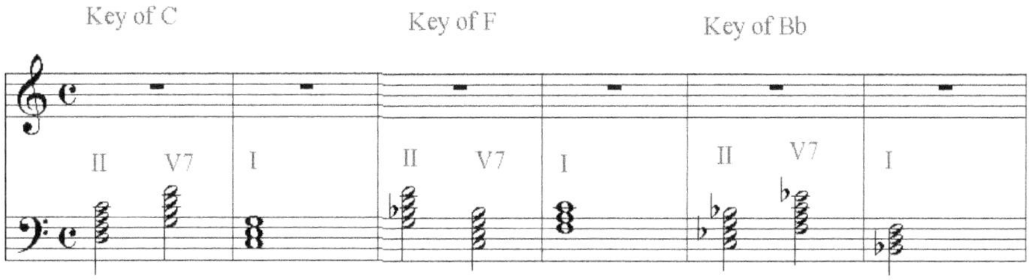

I hope you noticed something about this progression as you were thinking or playing through it. I hope you noticed that each chord is a 4th higher than the previous chord. In other words, in the Key of **C**, after the **D** chord is used, you go up a 4th (4 scale notes -- in terms of traditional harmony it is a "perfect 4th) to **G**. Then after the **G** chord is used, you go up a 4th to **C** to complete the cycle. If you didn't notice that, go back and play through these again.

Next lesson we'll meet another cousin, and see where she fits it to the scheme of things as far as chord prediction is concerned.

Chord Progressions Part Nine

The 'VI - II - V7 - I' Chord Progression

Last lesson we were introduced to "*cousin* **II**" -- the next most likely chord to occur in any given key after the primary chords **I**, **IV**, and **V**.

We said that cousin **II** might occur as a *major chord* or as a *minor chord* or as a *7th chord*, but however she appeared, she then almost always followed the chord progression of **II**, **V**, **I**. So once you meet cousin **II**, you pretty much know where she is going, don't you? She's almost always going to **V**, and **V** is almost always going to **I**.

If cousin **II** is in her 7th form, such as **II7** or **IIm7**, that even strengthens her predictability *more* -- those 7th chords REALLY want to move up a perfect 4th, for reasons we'll discuss later.

So if you're playing in the key of **C**, and you find yourself on a **Dm7** chord, you've got an 85% chance of predicting that the following chords will be **G** followed by **C**. You don't know when, of course, but just knowing the likely path gives you an *enormous advantage* over the musician who doesn't have a clue.

In this lesson, I would like to introduce you to another cousin. This time, "*cousin* **VI**." Cousin **VI** doesn't show up as often as cousin **II**, but she is terribly predictable. When she shows up, it is almost a slam dunk that she is going to move up a 4th to visit cousin **II**. She LOVES cousin **II**, and is pulled irresistibly toward her.

*Which means, of course, that when cousin **VI** shows up, you can predict with DEADLY ACCURACY what the next chord will be -- **II**. Close to 90% of the time **VI** moves to **II**. And you already know that **II** likes to move to **V**, and **V** likes to move to **I**, so.........*

The **VI** to **II** to **V** to **I** chord progression in each key is:

Key of **C**: **A D G C**

Key of **F**: **D G C F**

Key of **G**: **E A D G**

Key of **D**: **B E A D**

Key of **A**: **F# B E A**

Key of **E**: **C# F# B E**

Key of **B**: **G# C# F# B**

Key of **Gb**: **Eb Ab Db Gb**

Key of **Db**: **Bb Eb Ab Db**

Key of **Eb**: **C F Bb Eb**

Key of **Ab**: **F Bb Eb Ab**

Key of **Bb**: **G C F B**

And here's what it looks like in printed notation:

You'll notice immediately that each progression is up a perfect 4th (or down a perfect 5th -- same thing). You may be smelling something called the *"Circle of 4ths"* coming up. **You're right.**

Chord Progressions Part Ten

The 'Blue Moon' Chord Progression

In the lesson before last we learned the most obvious chord progression of all:

The "**Oh Duh**" Chord Progression

1. If there are 3 primary chords in a key -- **I**, **IV**, and **V** -- *and there are*;
2. And since most songs start and end on the **I** chord -- *and they do*;
3. Then the obvious conclusion is that there are *only two* possibilities for the next chord -- the **V** chord or the **IV** chord;
4. So if the melody note *is part of the* **V** *chord*, then the chord is *probably the* **V** *chord.* (**Duh!**) If the melody note *is part of the* **IV** *chord*, then the chord is *probably the* **IV** *chord.* (**Duh!**)

Just to briefly review, here they are again -- the 3 most used chords -- the primary chords -- in each major key:

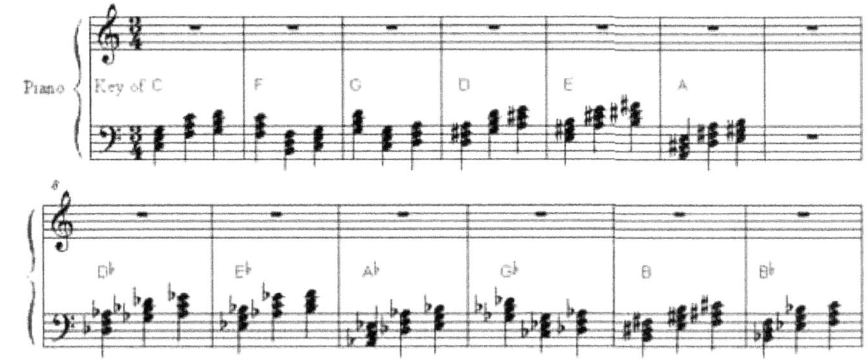

Then we learned the "creep" chord progression:

Creeping up by 1/2 steps until a
stable chord is reached - F - a primary chord.

Once the progression reaches a stable chord -- usually a primary chord -- then it can be combined with one or more other progressions to create an entire song.

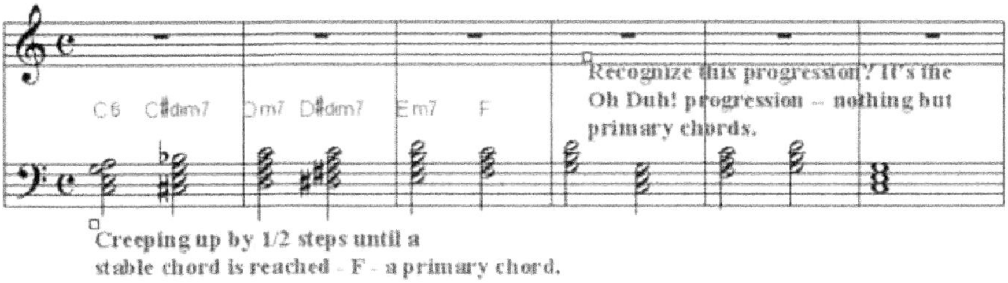
C6 C#dim7 Dm7 D#dim7 Em7 F
Recognize this progression? It's the Oh Duh! progression -- nothing but primary chords.
Creeping up by 1/2 steps until a stable chord is reached - F - a primary chord.

Then we learned that 2 or more chord progressions can be *combined* in one song. That gives the song a **form**. And forms are named such as:

Theme - Theme - *Contrast* - Theme

This form is known as **A A B A** musical form.

If the song went like this:

Theme - *Contrast* - Theme

...it would be known as **A B A** musical form.

Can you guess what this might be called?

Theme - *Contrast* - Theme - *Contrast* - Theme - *Contrast* - Theme - *Contrast*

Right you are! **A B A B** form.

Can you think of a book of songs made mostly out of **A B A B** form songs?

Sure. A hymnbook. Verse 1, chorus, Verse 2, chorus, Verse 3, chorus, etc. Whether a hymn has 1 verse or many verses, as long as it has a verse-chorus form it is called **A B A B** form.

Since every song has a form of some kind, so you can do yourself a **HUGE favor** and begin to look at songs with an eye to figuring out their musical form!

Why?

Because if you can recognize a song as an **A A B A** form song, all you have to do is determine the chord progression of the "**A**" section, and you've *automatically* learned 3/4 of the song! All that remains is learning the "**B**" section, and ***you've got it***!

This lesson I want to share with you the *most-used* chord progression in the world, bar none. It's been called the "*We Want Cantor*" progression, the "*Blue Moon*" progression, the "*Heart and Soul*" progression, and other names. I'm going to call it the "*2 kids at a piano*" progression.

> *The reason I call it that is because when I was a kid I used to play this progression (long before I knew what a progression was!) as a duet along with my brother, or my cousin, or a friend. I'm not a kid anymore, and yet I still hear that progression over and over and over again anytime there is a piano sitting around and a couple kids in the room. One kid takes the top part (the melody), and the other kid plays the bottom part (the chord progression).*

You've heard it too. *At least a* **zillion** *times*. The formula is easy: **I VI II V**

In other words, one measure of the **I** chord, one measure of the **VI** chord, one measure of the **II** chord, and one measure of the **V** chord. And then repeat as many times as you want, or until some adult says "Would you kids *please* stop banging on that piano?"

Blue Moon Progression:

I vi7 ii7 V7

*So in the key of **C**, that would translate to:*

I=C VI=A II=D V=G

*In the key of **F**:*

I=F VI=D II=G V=C

*In the key of **G**:*

I=G VI=E II=A V=D

*In the key of **D**:*

I=D VI=B II=E V=A

*In the key of **A**:*

I= A VI=F# II=B V=E

*In the key of **E**:*

I= E VI=C# II=F# V=B

*In the key of **Bb**:*

I=Bb VI=G II=C V=F

*In the key of **Eb**:*

I=Eb VI=C II=F V=Bb

*In the key of **Ab**:*

I=Ab VI=F II=Bb V=Eb

*In the key of **Db**:*

I=Db VI=Bb II=Eb V=Ab

*In the key of **Gb**:*

I=Gb VI=Eb II=Ab V=Db

*In the key of **B**:*

I=B VI=G# II=C# V=F#

(And of course, the same would be true in enharmonic keys such as **C#**, **F#**, and so on.)

There are *many variations* to this progression. Usually the two "middle chords -- the **VI** and the **II** -- are played as minor chords, and are then known as **vi** and **ii** (use *small* Roman numerals for *minor chords*). Usually, too, all the chords except the **I** chord have a 7th in them --in other words, in the key of **C**:

C Am7 Dm7 G7

Next lesson we'll look at some variations by using "*embedded chord subs*" in the Blue Moon progression. See you then.

Chord Progressions Part 11

Embedded Chord Subs In The 'Blue Moon' Chord Progression

Last lesson we learned the "*Blue Moon*" chord progression. Here's a brief review:

The "Blue Moon" chord progression

The formula is easy: **I VI II V**

In other words, one measure of the **I** chord, one measure of the **VI** chord, one measure of the **II** chord, and one measure of the **V** chord. And then repeat as many times as you want, or until some adult says "Would you kids *please* stop banging on that piano?"

Blue Moon Progression:

I vi7 ii7 V7

*So in the key of **C**, that would translate to:*

I=C VI=A II=D V=G

*In the key of **F**:*

I=F VI=D II=G V=C

*In the key of **G**:*

I=G VI=E II=A V=D

*In the key of **D**:*

I=D VI=B II=E V=A

*In the key of **A**:*

I= A VI=F# II=B V=E

*In the key of **E**:*

I= E VI=C# II=F# V=B

*In the key of **Bb**:*

I=Bb VI=G II=C V=F

*In the key of **Eb**:*

I=Eb VI=C II=F V=Bb

*In the key of **Ab**:*

I=Ab VI=F II=Bb V=Eb

*In the key of **Db**:*

I=Db VI=Bb II=Eb V=Ab

*In the key of **Gb**:*

I=Gb VI=Eb II=Ab V=Db

*In the key of **B**:*

I=B VI=G# II=C# V=F#

(And of course, the same would be true in enharmonic keys such as **C#**, **F#**, and so on.)

There are *many variations* to this progression. Usually the two "middle chords -- the **VI** and the **II** -- are played as minor chords, and are then known as **vi** and **ii** (use small Roman numerals for minor chords). Usually, too, all the chords except the **I** chord have a 7th in them --in other words, in the key of **C**:

C Am7 Dm7 G7

You can experiment around and find combinations you like -- you're not obligated to use the *same exact chords* as everyone else!

How to "embed chord subs" between the main chords

You know by now, too, that you can use 1/2 step slides as connective chords between the main chords. For example, if I was playing the progression listed above, I might insert a **Bb7** between **C** and **Am7** as a chord substitution. That would let me "*slide in*" to **Am7** in a smooth fashion. Then I might slide into the next chord -- **Dm7** -- from 1/2 step above -- **Ebm7**. Or I might slide into **G7** -- **Ab7** to **G7**. Or I might slide into **C** the second time around: **G7 Db7 C**.

So starting with this:

C Am7 Dm7 G7

Which looks like this when notated:

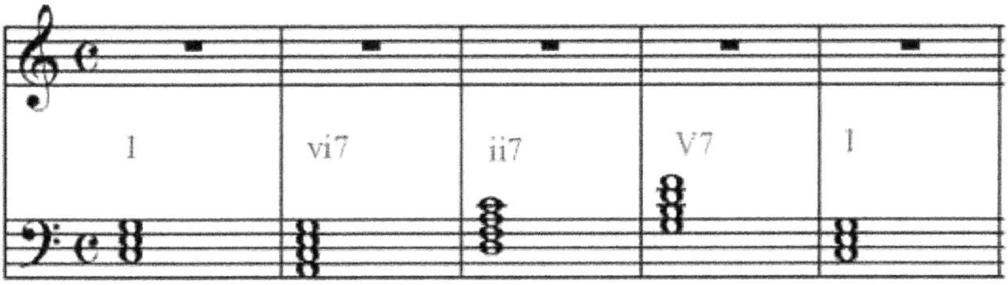

.....I might end up with this:

C Bb7 Am7 Eb7 Dm7 Gb7 G7 Db7 C

Quite a difference! Here's what it looks like in notation in the key of **C**:

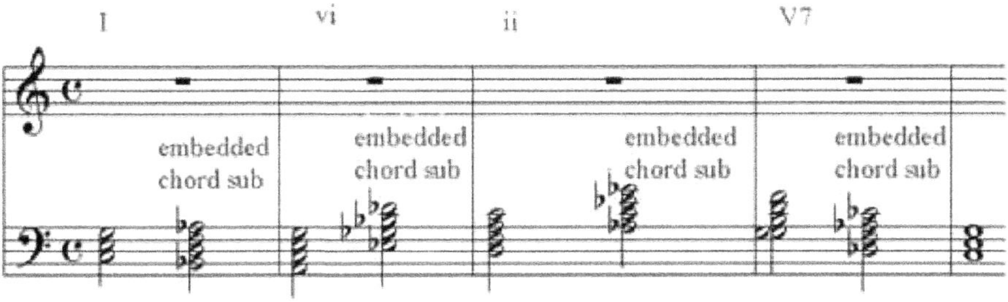

Experiment around and see what you can come up with. Slide up to chords and down to chords. Make some minor and some major. Add 7ths, add 9ths.

But whatever you do, **get this chord progression down cold** so you can play it in any key, and recognize it when you hear it. It's used in a thousand songs, and you can be sure that it will continue to be used in the future in *new* and *creative* ways!

Chord Progressions Part Twelve

The '12 Bar Blues' Chord Progression

Far and away the most-used chord progression of all time in the world of jazz and blues and rhythm & blues (and even much of rock and fusion) is the 12-bar blues chord progression.

The 12-bar blues is all-American. It developed right here, and until the last few years, it's main musicians were right here in the US.

I had the privilege not long ago of standing on the corner of Bourbon St. and listening to the musicians in Preservation Hall play some of the most authentic blues I've heard.

You simply play 12 measures of the same chord progression over and over, each time improvising some different melody on top of those changes. And those changes are:

The 12 Bar Blues Chord Progression

4 bars of the **I** chord

2 bars of the **IV** chord

2 bars of the **I** chord

1 bar of the **V** chord

1 bar of the **IV** chord

2 bars of the **I** chord

The 7th is usually added to each chord -- so if the **I** chord is **F**, you would usually play **F7** -- that is kind of assumed in the blues.

As you can see, the structure of the 12 bar blues is very simple. And since it is fun, play it over and over again until you get the sounds you want!

The "*melody*" of the 12-bar blues is something that each musician makes up as he/she goes along. It is based on the *blues scale*, which is a bit different than the regular diatonic scale we all grew up with -- it includes all those "*regular*" notes, but also uses the *flat 3rd*, the *flat 5th*, and the *flat 7th* degrees of the scale.

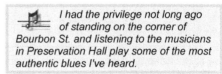

Here is the blues scale in the key of **C**:

The "*blues scale*" is really a combination of the major diatonic scale (the "*regular*" scale we all grew up with) plus three additional notes:

The **flatted 3rd**;

The **flatted 5th** (or sharp 4th -- same thing);

The **flatted 7th**

So the blues scale really contains *11 notes* -- the 8 of the normal diatonic scale -- and the 3 "blue notes." These are used in various combinations, as we shall see, to create a "*bluesy sound.*"

The blues started not as a piano style, but as a vocal style, and of course the human voice can sing "*in the cracks*" between the notes on the keyboard. So when we play blues on the keyboard, we try to imitate the human voice by playing BOTH the *3rd* and the *flat 3rd* -- BOTH the *5th* and the *flat 5th* -- BOTH the *7th* and the *flat 7th.*

We would play in the cracks if we could, but we can't, so we do the best we can by combining the intervals to imitate the quarter steps that a human voice can sing.

Certain instruments can do that too -- for example, the trombone. Since it has a slide, it can hit an infinite number of tones between any two keyboard notes.

Later we'll have a lesson on voicing the 12 bar blues, but for now, just learn the form and practice it in all the keys.

Chord Progressions Part 13

Enlarging the '12 Bar Blues' Chord Progression Through the Use of 'Embedded Chord Subs'

Last time we learned the 12-bar blues progression -- hope you have it down cold by now, as you will use it your entire musical life in scads of songs -- many of them not even known as "blues" songs.

In this lesson we're going to learn how we can make the 12-bar blues progression much more interesting and complex through the use of *embedded chord subs.*

Let's look first at some chord substitutions we can insert into the skeleton, and then take a look at creating a melody to go with the chords.

First of all, remember to use *7ths* on all the **I**, **IV**, and **V** chords -- in other words, **I7**, **IV7**, and **V7**. That will give you are more "*bluesy*" sound right off the bat. Then to that add some 9ths for a fuller sound. For example, let's say you're playing the blues in **Bb**. To the **I** chord you would add a 7th, which of course is **Ab**. If you add a 9th for fullness, that would be a **C**. So the chord would be made up of **Bb**, **D**, **F**, **Ab**, and **C**. One way to voice this chord would be to play a low **Bb** on the first beat, then on subsequent beats play a chord made up of **F**, **Ab**, **C**, and **D**. On the **IV** chord, that would translate to a low **Eb**, then **Bb**, **Db**, **F**, and **G**. On the **V** chord it would be a low **F**, then **C**, **Eb**, **F**, and **G**.

Next, use some *half-step slides* as chord subs. For example, as you move from the **I** chord to the **IV** chord, you could "*slide in*" to the **IV** chord by playing the 7th or 9th chord 1/2 step above the target chord -- in other words, **E7** or **E9th** to **Eb7th** or **9th**. It's like sliding into a base in baseball: you play the chord 1/2 step higher on the 4th beat (or even on the "and" after the 4th beat) as you move to the next chord. As you move from **F7** to **Bb7**, you could play **B7th** on the 4th beat of the measure right before you play **Bb7th**.

Another chord substitution would be to use a *suspension* on any one of the primary chords before resolving to the chord itself. For example, let's say you are playing the **Bb7** chord but your next chord is **Eb7**. Instead of playing **Eb7th** right away, play **Eb7sus** for one or two beats before resolving to **Eb7**.

You can do that on any of the chords, and it adds lots of interest to the progression because of the variety and also because of the suspense a suspension creates before it is resolved.

Another way to create a chord substitution is to substitute a *minor 7th* chord a perfect 4th lower than the 7th chord being used, then resolve to the 7th chord. For example, before playing **Eb7**, play **Bbm7th** as a chord sub (it is a perfect 4th lower than **Eb7**), then resolve to **Eb7**. The time frame is always up to you -- I usually hold a sus a beat or two before moving on.

Still another chord sub is to ask yourself this question: "*Into what other 7th chord will this melody note fit?*" For example, let's say your melody is **D**, and the chord under it is **Bb7**. By asking yourself the question listed above, you might come up with **D7** or **G7**. Use one of them as a chord sub for **Bb7**. The possibilities are endless.

Now let's consider how to create a melody to go with the blues progression. Most beginners make the mistake of playing too many notes too fast, and not taking time to think. It's better to pick a short motif and develop it.

For example, if the chord is **Bb7**, pick *3 or 4 notes* that more or less go with the chord, and make a simple motif out of them. (Motif means "*theme*"). You could take 3 notes such as **F**, **G**, and **D**, and play them in various orders and various rhythms until some repetitive theme occurs. When it does, build on that theme by changing chords and repeating the same motif, but at a different point on the scale.

*For example, if your motif was **F**, **F**, **D**, **G**, **F**, **D** while the chord was **Bb7**, you could "rhyme the motif" by playing **Bb**, **Bb**, **G**, **C**, **Bb**, **G** while the chord is **Eb7**. (Words make it complicated -- it's really easy -- which is why we publish most all our courses on video so you can see and understand quickly!).*

Chord Progressions Part 14

The 'Alternating 7ths & m7th Chords' Chord Progression

Back a few lessons we learned about the "*Circle of Keys*" -- also called the "*Circle of 4ths*", or the "*Circle of 5ths*". Let's take a review of that:

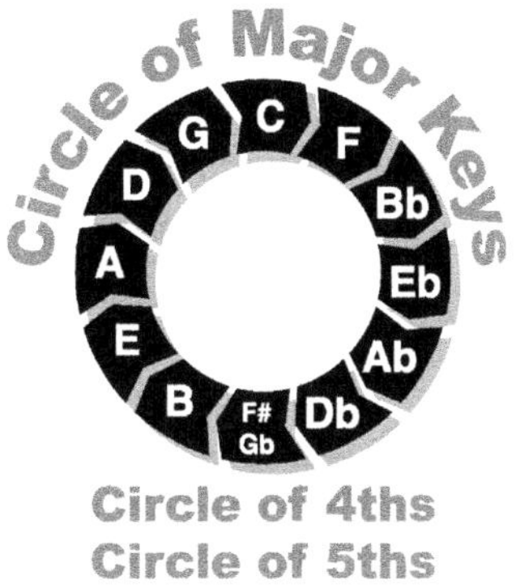

If you've ever heard of the "*circle of 4ths*" or the "*circle of 5ths*", they are the same thing as the "*circle of keys*." It just depends on whether you're moving clockwise or counter-clockwise around the circle.

All the major keys that you can play in -- 12 of 'em -- are listed in this circle. Take a look for yourself:

Major Keys:

C F Bb Eb Ab Db Gb B E A D G

So "**C**" is at the top of your circle, and **Gb** (same as **F#**) is at the bottom of your circle.

Now memorize that circle. You'll soon notice that each letter is a *4th above* the previous letter -- hence, the "*circle of 4ths*." Or if you go the other way, you'll soon notice that each letter is a 5th above the previous letter -- hence, the "*circle of 5ths*."

> *This is the way chords "want" to move -- up a 4th. Or up a 5th. You will find those to be the most common chord progression of all -- up a 4th from the previous chord, or up a 5th from the previous chord.*

For example, if the chord you are playing is **C**, the most likely chord to occur next is either **F** or **G**. You will notice that **F** comes directly to the right of **C** on the circle, and **G** directly to the left. (And you do remember, don't you, that **C**, **F**, and **G** are the "*family chords*" of the **Key of C**? -- the primary chords -- therefore, the most likely chords to occur? -- Now you know why!)

So that means that at any point on the circle you can immediately know the most likely chords -- the chord to the left, and the chord to the right! Here's a quiz:

What are the 3 most likely chords in the key of **Db**?

Right.

Db (of course), plus the chords on either side of it -- **Ab** and **Gb**.

So what we come out with is this -- the most likely chords in each key:

Do you see what an enormous advantage this gives you? You have a *highly educated guess* what chords are going to occur in the song you are playing based on the key that the song is written in. Not only that, you now know that chords like to either move up a 4th or a 5th (or down a 4th or 5th -- same thing).

And so as we begin learning chord progressions, this is the first step -- memorize the circle above until you can say it forward and backward and upside down and in your sleep! If I were you, I would print it out and stick it up on your piano or bathroom mirror or wherever you would see it often -- ***it's that important***.

But there are also *12 minor keys* in which songs can be written, so there must also be a circle of minor keys. It's not as well known as the circle of major keys, but it works the same way. Here it is:

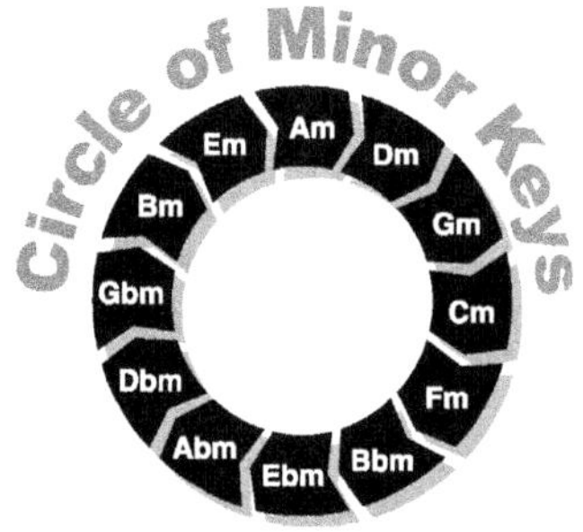

It works the same way as the major circle of keys, *with one exception*:

When figuring the 3 most likely chords in any key, you still look left and look right, but because of the fact that most songs written in the western hemisphere use the harmonic minor scale instead of the natural minor scale (which is much too involved to get into here -- if you want to know about that in detail you'll need to get a course on scales), the chord to the left is usually a MAJOR chord instead of a minor chord.

So in the key of **Am**, the 3 most likely chords would be **Am**, **Dm**, and ***E major*** -- not ***E minor***! There are some exceptions to that, but not many.

So what we come out with is this -- the most likely chords in each minor key:

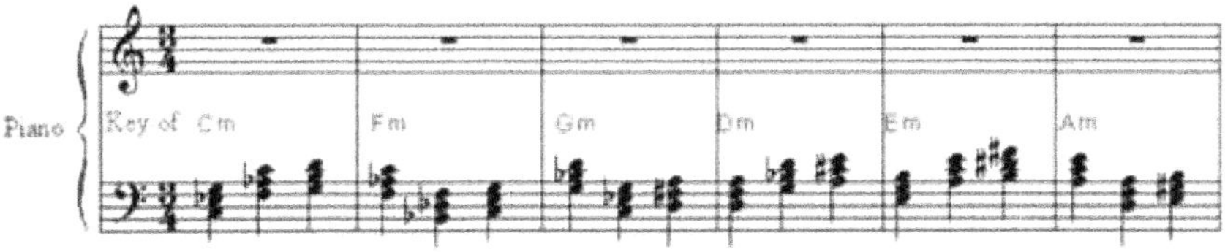

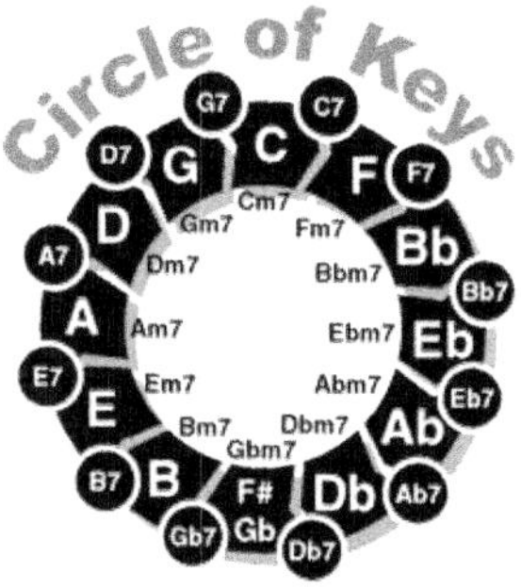

Now what we are going to do is combine the two circles and add 7ths to each chord:

You'll notice that between each of the 12 chords there is a 7th chord which connects one chord to the next chord as you move around the circle counter-clockwise. There is also a minor 7th chord which could be played as an alternative to the major chord.

Now -- here's the deal:

Thousands and thousands and thousands of songs have a section of this circle embedded in them! Not *all* the circle -- just *part* of the circle.

For example, in the song "*All The Things You Are*", the right-hand part of the circle is being used from **F** to **Db**. Go to your piano and play these chords:

Fm7 Bbm7 Eb7 Ab Db

You will recognize those chords as the chord progression used in that particular song. The progression simply followed the circle around 5/12th of the way! If you knew about the circle of keys, that would be completely logical to you, and you would pick it up in a flash. If you didn't know the circle, you might think they were just random chords!

Can you begin to see and understand why knowing chords and chord progressions is so critically important?

Then in the very next phrase of the same song the progression goes like this:

Cm7 Fm7 Bb7 Eb Ab

Hmmm. *Does that ring a bell?*

Sure. Another progression moving 5/12th of the way around the circle.

That's how songs are made -- combining one progression with another. Usually, though, songs only have 3 or 4 sets of progressions, and those progressions usually repeat within the song. So if you grasp the progression the first time it happens, you are looking for it to occur again, and you won't be surprised when it happens.

Do you know the old song "*Please don't talk about me when I'm gone*"? It uses this same progression. Here's the theme:

Ab   C7   F7   Bb7   Eb7   Ab

After starting on **Ab**, the composer jumps across the circle to **C7**, then predictably follows the circle 5/12ths of the way around the circle.

> *If you're wondering if this only happens in popular music, get a copy of " Liebestraum" by Lizst, and you'll find exactly the same chord progression! In fact, you could play that section of Liebestraum at the same time you're playing "Please don't talk about me when I'm gone", and the chords would match perfectly. (I'm not suggesting you do this except at home -- taste is a different matter!)*

Chord Progressions Part 15

How To Create Unlimited Original Chord Progressions Using Chord Substitutions

Chord Subs Technique #1
The "What Other Chord?" Technique

The "*What Other Chord?*" technique is one of the best ways to create a fresh harmonization of a familiar melody.

You simply ask yourself: "In to what other chord will this melody note fit?"

For example, the melody of "*Silent Night*" (if we play it in the key of **C**) goes like this:

G A G E

In the original score, the chord under this melody is **C** major. But are we obligated to keep the original harmony? *Not at all.* If we decide to go with **C** major on the first measure, we may want to change the chord in the 2nd measure just for variety. But to *what chord*?

That's where our "*What other chord?*" technique comes in. We simply ask ourselves "Into what other chord will this melody note -- namely **E** -- fit?" Let's see: In the **C** chord, **E** is the 3rd of the chord, so:

E is the *root* of the **E** chord, so we could try **E**, or **Em**, or **Em7**, or any other kind of "**E**" chord.

E is the *5th* of the **A** chord, so we could try **A**, or **Am**, or **Am7**, or any other kind of "**A**" chord.

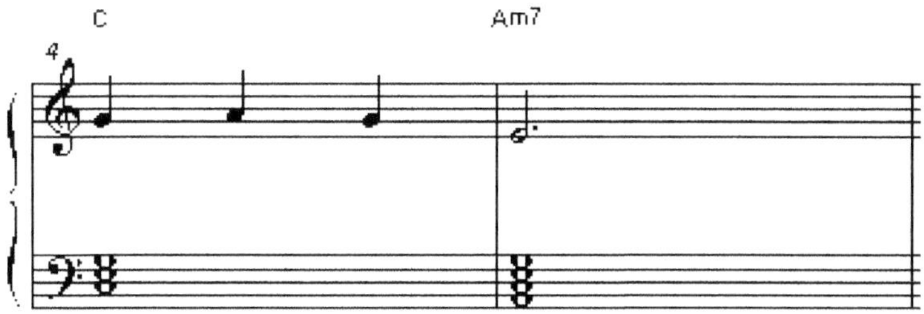

E is the *7th* of the **F** chord, so we could try **Fmaj7**, or **Fm/maj7**, or **F+/maj7**, etc. -- any "**F**" chord with an **E** in it.

E is the *9th* of the **D** chord, so we could try **D9**, or **Dm9**, or any "**D**" chord with an **E** in it.

Get the idea?

Next lesson we will demonstrate another chord substitution technique.

Chord Progressions Part 16

How To Create Unlimited Original Chord Progressions Using Chord Substitutions

Chord Subs Technique #2
The "m7 down a 4th for 7th" Chord Substitution Technique

The "m7 down a 4th for 7th" technique is another of the best ways to create a fresh harmonization of a familiar melody.

Here's the deal:

For any *7th chord*, substitute a *minor 7th* chord a *perfect 4th lower*, if the melody will tolerate it.

For example, the 2nd chord in "*Silent Night*" (if we play it in the key of **C**) is the **G7** chord. So we simply go down a perfect 4th from **G** -- which is **D** -- and we build a minor 7th chord. The melody at that point is "**D**", so there's no conflict between the melody and the chord. *So it works*. After playing **Dm7**, we can go back to **G7**. We have just made the song more interesting.

If you're not sure what chord is a perfect 4th below a 7th, here's a chord substitution chart that will help you. You might want to print it out and keep it on your music rack on your piano:

7th chord -----	m7 chord subs	7th chord -----	m7 chord subs
C7	**Gm7**	**B7**	**F#m7**
F7	**Cm7**	**Db7**	**Abm7**
G7	**Dm7**	**Eb7**	**Bbm7**
D7	**Am7**	**Ab7**	**Ebm7**
A7	**Em7**	**Gb7**	**Dbm7**
E7	**Bm7**	**Bb7**	**Fm7**

So:

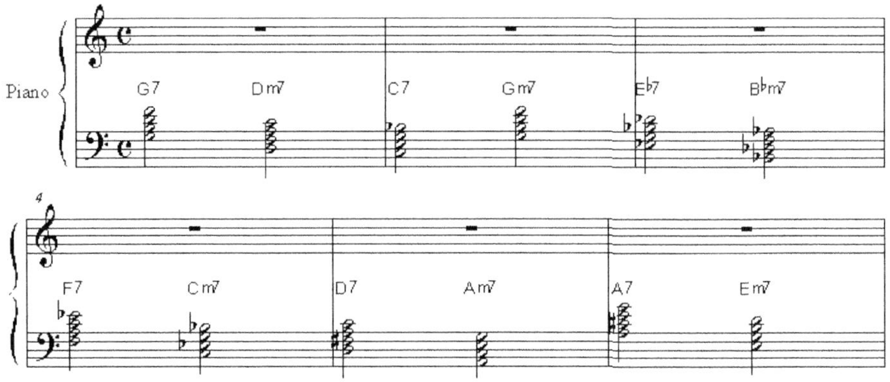

Get the idea?

Next lesson we will demonstrate another chord substitution technique.

Chord Progressions Part 17

How To Create Unlimited Original Chord Progressions Using Chord Substitutions

Chord Subs Technique #3
The "Half-Step Slide" Chord Substitution Technique

The "*half-step slide*" technique is another of the best ways to create a fresh harmonization of a familiar melody.

Here's how it works:

Slide into the target chord by playing the chord 1/2 step above or below it.

For example, the 2nd chord in "*Silent Night*" (if we play it in the key of **C**) is the **G7** chord. So we play the chord 1/2 step above **G7** -- which is **Ab7** -- and "slide into" **G7**. The next chord after that is **C**, so we can play **Db7** right before **C** if you want to. Then the next chord – the target chord -- is **F**, so 1/2 step above **F** is **Gb7**, and we can slide into **F** by playing that first.

Could we slide up instead of slide down? Sure -- it just depends on the melody note -- sometimes a slide up sounds better with the melody, and sometimes a slide down sounds better with the melody. We have to do some trial and error to find out, but once we find what works, we can use it over and over. So by doing this we have just made the song a lot more interesting.

Get the idea?

So now we have learned 3 of the most powerful chord substitution techniques known to man (or women, for that matter):

1. The "*Into what other chord will this melody note fit?*" technique.
2. The "*m7 down a 4th for 7th*" technique.
3. The "*half-step slide*" technique.

Chord Progressions Part 18

The "Get On That Church!" Gospel Progression Also known as "4 of the 4" chord progression

When I was a young piano player in Los Angeles I used to love to go to a jazz club out on the Sunset Strip in Hollywood known as "The Bit." It was a tiny little place -- I doubt if it seated more than 50 people -- yet it was THE place for jazz fans (such as Wilt "The Stilt" Chamberlain, who frequented the place and seated himself in the tiny venue by throwing one leg completely over a table!) to hang out and see the great jazz artists of that era. I vividly recall sitting at a little table with Bev, my new bride, and chatting with Anita O'Day and Helen Forrest, two great female jazz singers. I was a fan of Anita at the time, but I didn't know who Helen was (I was a bit too young). Later I found out that she sang with several of the big bands of the '40's including Benny Goodman and Harry James and appeared with Bob Hope and company as they entertained the troops during WW II.

I was taking piano lessons back then from THE piano teacher in Hollywood -- Dave R........., who had a little studio on Cahuenga Blvd, which was between Hollywood Blvd and Sunset. All the big names of that era took lessons from Dave, and I would meet them as I was coming or leaving Dave's studio. One of the pianists I met was a talented and playful guy named Les, who occasionally played at The Bit. He went on to become a very big name in jazz. If you are a jazz fan, you no doubt know his last name, which I won't mention here, at least until I get his permission (I haven't talked with him in years.)

Les used a technique which I have never forgotten -- I don't remember what he called it -- but I have named it "*Get On That Church*" (in case that phrase doesn't make sense to you, here's a rough translation: "You kids get on down to the church -- you hear!") chord progression, which as I recall was also the name of one of his original tunes. Here is what it is:

Gospel Technique #1
"Get On That Church!" Chord Progression

The **IV** chord of the **IV** chord, *followed by*

the **IV** chord, *followed by*

the **I** chord.

Let's spell it out to make it clear. Pretend you're in the Key of C. The I chord is C -- correct? And the IV chord is F -- correct? Now --

what chord is a perfect 4th higher than F? Just count up the F scale 4 notes - F, G, A, Bb. So the answer is Bb. That's the IV of the IV

chord. So the progression in the Key of C would be: Bb to F to C.

Here's what it would look like in each key:

*Key of **C***	*Key of **Eb***	*Key of **D***
Bb to **F** to **C**	**Db** to **Ab** to **Bb**	**C** to **G** to **D**
*Key of **F#***	*Key of **F***	*Key of **Ab***
E to **B** to **F#**	**Eb** to **Bb** to **F**	**Gb** to **Db** to **Ab**
*Key of **A***	*Key of **B***	*Key of **G***
G to **D** to **A**	**A** to **E** to **B**	**F** to **C** to **G**
*Key of **Db***	*Key of **E***	*Key of **Bb***
Cb to **Gb** to **Db**	**D** to **A** to **E**	**Ab** to **Eb** to **Bb**

But here's the *key* to giving it a "*gospel sound*" -- use the 1st inversion of the first chord (the **IV** chord of the **IV** chord), the 2nd inversion of the 2nd chord (the **IV** chord), and the root position of the last chord (**I**). You can either use the root of each chord as your *left hand low note*, or you can use the root of the **I** chord as an *ostinato* (constant low note).

It's also fine to embed a 7th in any or all of the chords -- the "bluesier" the better!

Next lesson we will demonstrate another gospel technique, which builds on this technique, but turns it into a rock or jazz riff.

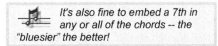

Chord Progressions Part 19

The "Walk On Up" Gospel Progression

Last lesson we looked at a chord progression that is technically known as a "*double plagel cadence*." A plagel cadence is a chord progression that closes a section of music with a **IV** to **I**. A double plagel cadence would mean playing the **IV** of the **IV** before ending on the **I** chord:

This time we will demonstrate another gospel technique, which builds on this technique, but turns it into a rock or jazz riff. We'll call it the "*walk on up*" chord progression, because it "walks up a 4th" to the next chord, and then uses the "IV of IV" chord progression for a bluesy feel.

Gospel Technique #2 "Walk On Up!" Chord Progression

Walk in 10ths from the **I** chord up to the **IV** chord, but quickly move to the **IV** of the **IV** first, then back to the **IV**, then back to the **I** chord. Use 7ths freely.

Here's an example in the key of **Bb**.

You can toggle back and forth all day long on those 3 chords -- the **I7** chord (put a 7th in all chords to make them sound bluesy), the **IV7** chord, and the **IV7** of the **IV7** chord. Many gospel players use very little else except variations of these 3 chords. Of course there are many other techniques you could use, but it would take another entire book to chronicle all the potential techniques available.

But for the purposes of this book, this is plenty, and will keep you playing variations of this for *years to come*!

Review time!

We've come to the end of our 39 lessons, so it's time to do some review so we can see the entire picture in context.

Let me begin by asking you a question:

"Why would anyone want to learn chords or chord progressions?"

The short answer is "*understanding.*" By learning chords and how they are formed and used, we are getting inside of music to see what it is made of.

> *It's like having an x-ray machine that looks deep inside of an object, to see what makes that object tick.*

And by learning chord progressions, we see how composers link chords together into meaningful segments called "*phrases*" and "*sections.*"

The long answer is that chords and progressions contribute to making a musician complete. It's great to be able to read music, and we certainly should pursue that goal. But if we are lost without music, then we need some music theory understanding to fill in the gaps in our knowledge and understanding.

There's a famous story about a world-class concert pianist who when asked to play "*Happy Birthday*" at a friends' home couldn't do it because there was no sheet music available for it in that home. That's an extreme and pathetic example, but many lesser embarrassments happen every day around the world because piano players don't know theory and don't understand how chords tie everything together.

Well, there's no need for YOU to ever fall into that trap, because in 39 lessons we have covered a ton of subjects. Here's a quick review:

All 12 of the Major Chords

All 12 of the Minor Chords

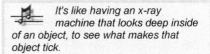

Diminished Triads

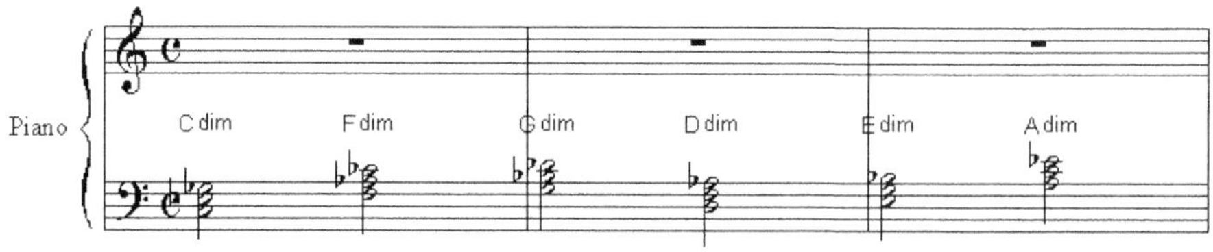

Augmented Triads

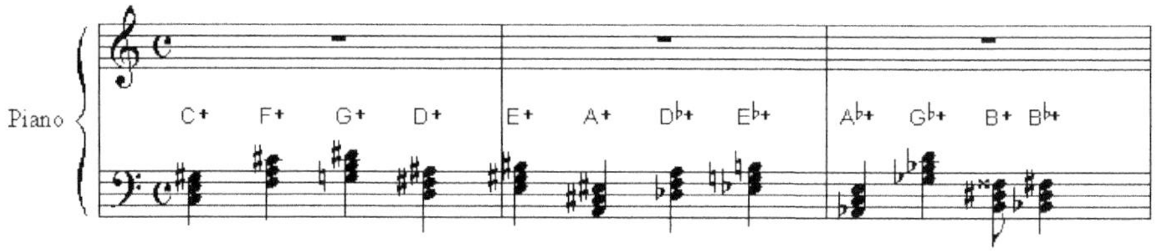

All the 6th chords

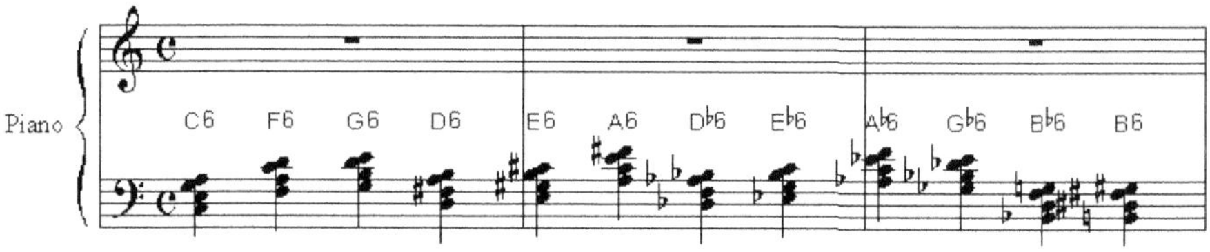

All the Minor 6th chords

7th chords

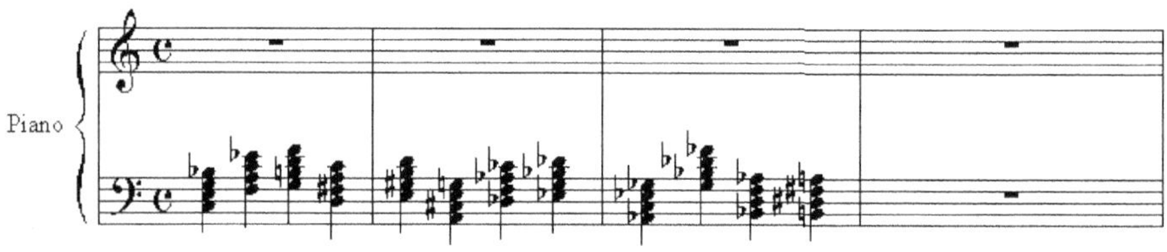

Maj7th chords

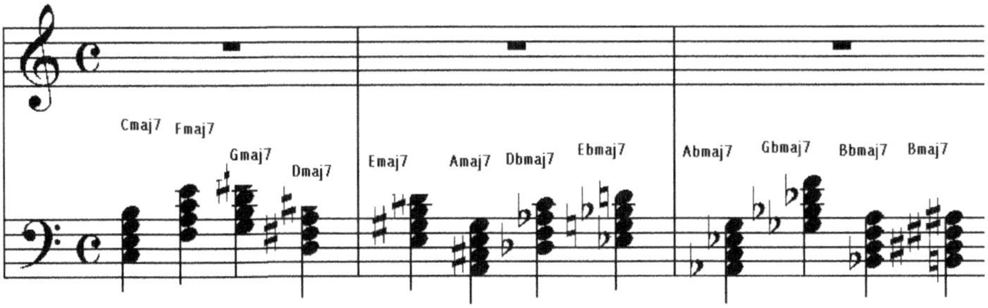

Minor 7th chords

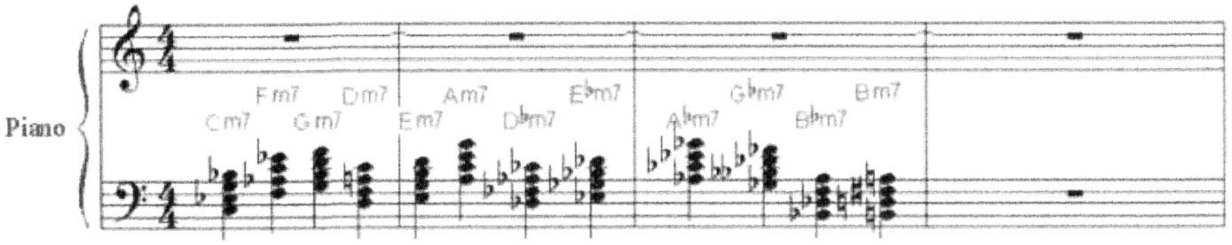

All the 9th chords

11th chords

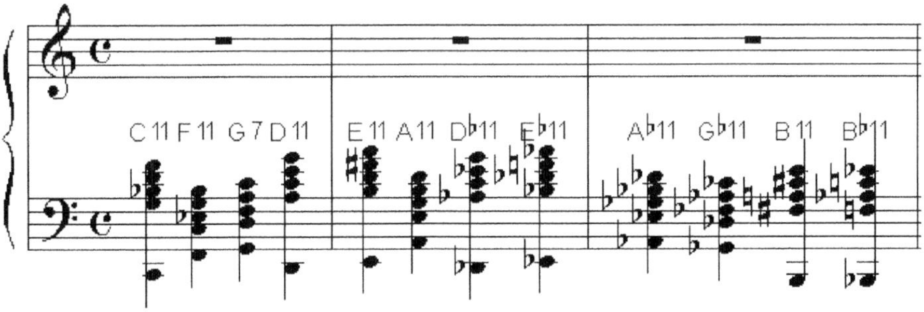

All the 13th chords

Suspensions

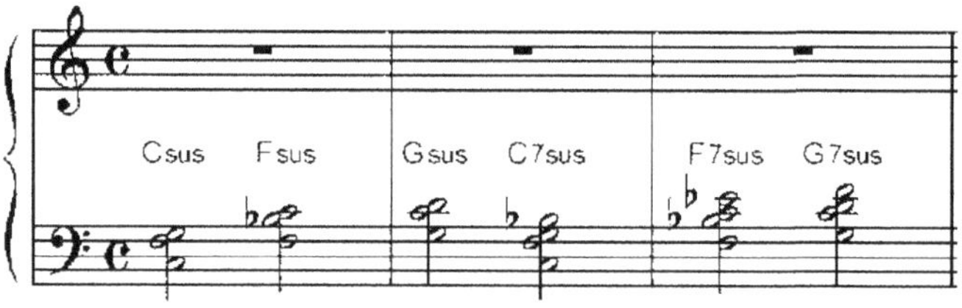

Then we learned that there were also *alterations* and *slash chords* -- way too many to list here, because actually there is no limit to the combinations of alterations and slash chords when combined!

Then along the way we learned a little about musical forms -- such forms as **ABA**, **AABA**, **ABCA**, and so on. And we learned how the "*Circle of Keys*" (also known as the "*Circle of 4ths*" and "*Circle of 5ths*") impacted chord progressions because of the proclivity of chords to move up a perfect 4th. We also learned that there is a "*Circle of Minor Keys*", and then we combined the major circle with the minor circle to create some interesting progressions.

Once we covered chords, we got into chord progressions, and here are some of the ones we covered:

The "**Oh Duh!**" Chord Progression

The "*Creep*" Chord Progression

The "*Blue Moon*" Chord Progression

The "*12 Bar Blues*" Chord Progression

...and we learned how embedded chord subs could make a progression lots more interesting, and we learned the 3 most important rules of chord substitutions.

Are there other progressions?

Of course. But these are the *biggies* -- the progressions you will run into time and time again.

And so we have come to the end of our time together. I hope you have enjoyed our journey as much as I have.

Thanks again, and blessings on you!

Resources for Musicians

If you have enjoyed and profited musically from this book, then you will want to know about some other resources which are available to you:

www.playpiano.com -- Over 300 piano courses on DVD and CD

www.chordpiano.com -- 10 day course in "chord piano"

www.gospelpiano.com -- Praise & gospel piano playing

www.pianolesson.tv -- Piano runs & fills galore

www.pianoplayingbyear.com -- How to play the piano by ear

www.Pianoplayingwithchords.com -- Wonderful 7 month course in piano improvisation

www.pianolessonsbyvideo.com -- A Crash course in exciting piano for busy adults

www.pianoforbeginners.com -- Classical piano for beginning adults

www.keyboardchords.com -- Instant chord finder software for your computer desktop

www.pianoplaying.com -- How to dress up "naked music" on the piano

www.piano-playing-by-ear.com -- Piano playing secrets of the pros

www.pianomusicbyear.com -- How to *play* more notes without *reading* more notes

www.piano-music-chords.com -- How to arrange piano music on the spot as you play

www.chording-piano-music.com -- Portal site leading to hundreds of exciting music sites

www.home-business-music.com -- Turn your musical talent into an income stream through the 3 unique methods open to most all musicians

www.musical-instrument-review.com -- What to look for when you're in the market for a musical instrument

Printed in Great Britain
by Amazon

38099660R00057